Economic cycles

MANCHESTER
UNIVERSITY PRESS

Insights from Economic History
General editor: Nick Crafts

This series makes accessible major results from recent research in economic history with an emphasis on issues of current importance. The books present an authoritative and objective view of the 'lessons of history' for the non-expert, while comprising essential reference material for the professional economic historian. The focus of the series is on issues in economic history that have contemporary relevance for policy-makers and for economists wishing for a digest of key research results.

Already published

Tarrifs and growths
Forest Capie

Reconstructing Europe's trade and payments
Barry Eichengreen

Scotland and the UK
C. H. Lee

Economic cycles
Long cycles and business cycles since 1870

Solomos Solomou

Peterhouse, Cambridge and Faculty of Economics,
University of Cambridge

Manchester University Press
Manchester and New York
distributed exclusively in the USA by St. Martin's Press

Copyright © Solomos Solomou 1998

The right of Solomos Solomou to be identified as the author of this
work has been asserted by him in accordance with the Copyright,
Designs and Patents Act 1988.

Published by Manchester University Press
Oxford Road, Manchester M13 9NR, UK
and Room 400, 175 Fifth Avenue, New York, NY 10010, USA

Distributed exclusively in the USA by
St. Martin's Press, Inc., 175 Fifth Avenue, New York,
NY 10010, USA

Distributed exclusively in Canada by
UBC Press, University of British Columbia, 6344 Memorial Road,
Vancouver, BC, Canada V6T 1Z2

British Library Cataloguing-in-Publication Data
A catalogue record for this book is available from the British Library

Library of Congress Cataloging-in-Publication Data applied for

ISBN 0 7190 4150 3   *hardback*
0 7190 4151 1   *paperback*

First published 1998

02 01 00 99 98   10 9 8 7 6 5 4 3 2 1

Typeset by Ralph Footring, Derby
Printed by Bell & Bain Ltd, Glasgow

Γιά τον Νικολη μασ

Contents

Figures

Tables

Acknowledgements

In writing this book I have received valuable comments and advice from Nick Crafts and Michael Kitson. The book has also benefited from collaborative work with Luis Catao, Yougesh Khatri and Weike Wu. I would also like to thank the ESRC (grants R000221692 and R000221237) and the Nuffield Foundation for supporting my research.

Thanks are due to Nicola Viinikka and Pippa Kenyon of Manchester University Press for handling the book so efficiently. Ralph Footring copy-edited the book with clarity.

Chapter 1

Introduction

During the 1960s the literature on business cycles analysed 'the end of the business cycle' (Bronfenbrenner, 1969). Economists living in the 'golden age' of the post-war boom emphasised the success of **demand management** policies in stabilising economies. The Keynesian economic perspectives were seen to provide a basis for managing economies towards a path of stable economic growth, preventing extreme fluctuations such as those experienced in the inter-war era. The historical existence of business cycles was perceived as the outcome of a lack of economic insight. Such beliefs were challenged by the more marked economic fluctuations after 1973. These ideas (or perhaps hopes) seem even more anachronistic from the perspective of the 1990s, following the worst depression in 50 years. The more volatile business cycle movements since 1973 have given rise to a proliferation of business cycle theories in both the Keynesian and New Classical perspectives, revitalising business cycle discussions.

The most important lesson from this experience is that an historical perspective is essential if we are to understand how business cycles are generated and evolve. Economists analysing economic growth and fluctuations from a 1960s benchmark wrongly predicted the 'end of the business cycle'. An economist

1

looking at the period 1870–1913 from the 1913 benchmark would have predicted that economic cycles are fairly long, although not very severe in **amplitude**. Yet, what evolved in the inter-war era were extremely severe short fluctuations which had devastating effects on the world economy and national political institutions. Similarly, economists and policy makers looking back on the inter-war era from a 1938 perspective expected the future to be one of slow economic growth and a tendency towards deep depressions. Instead, the 'golden age' of 1950–73 was a unique episode of exceptionally rapid economic growth and mild **growth cycles**.

Such errors of prediction reflect naive expectation, which, in turn, reflects a simplistic theory of historical change. The general idea behind all these errors is that the present predicts the future. This has clearly not served us well. To argue that the current business cycle features (since 1973) will also be present in the future has no empirical or theoretical foundation. Only a long-run historical perspective, and theoretical structures that attempt to explain these observations, will allow us to make any sensible *conditional* predictions about the future. An historical perspective is important not because history repeats itself but because history illustrates the evolutionary nature of business cycle behaviour and gives us an understanding of the factors that generate change. In economic systems that entail behavioural, institutional, structural and policy changes, we can safely predict that business cycle features will not be stable. Once we can explain the observed inter-period changes in business cycle behaviour we shall be in a better position to understand the evolution of business cycles.

These observations also raise doubts about the general empirical approach in current business cycle research, the aim of which has been to explain the so-called 'stylised facts' of business cycles. Such approaches *assume* that regularities exist over time and across countries. However, these empirical regularities are usually derived from studies of very limited time periods (often the post-1960 era) and a small selection of countries (usually Britain and the US). If one of the descriptive features of business cycles, as will be argued in later chapters, is change over time, these empirical features cannot be seen to be universal stylised facts in time and space.

Even if we focus on a very limited set of empirical features, we observe important change over time. For example, consider the following three questions:

- What is the average period of the cycle?
- What is the average amplitude of the cycle?
- Do prices and output move together over the cycle?

Average cycle durations have changed over time (chapter 2). During 1870–1913 a number of variables (including aggregate investment, agricultural production and construction sector output) fluctuated with a **long swing** duration averaging about 20 years. During the inter-war period shorter fluctuations were observed. During the post-war 'golden age' the average cyclical period fell to five years. During the post-1973 era cycle durations have once again lengthened, averaging approximately ten years since the late 1970s. Cyclical amplitudes have also varied significantly over time. Low macroeconomic volatility during 1870–1913 gave way to high amplitude fluctuations during 1919–38; the stability of the post-war 'golden age' has been followed by the relatively more volatile post-1973 era. Much post-war research on business cycles has noted that prices and output have fluctuated **contra-cyclically** and has proceeded to explain this feature in terms of general business cycle theory. However, during the classical **gold standard** the relationship was not stable and during the inter-war period price and output fluctuations were **pro-cyclical**. *Assuming* universal stylised facts is not a realistic way of understanding business cycles.

The observed changes in business cycle behaviour also need to be integrated into a set of broader macroeconomic questions. For example, are mild economic fluctuations outcomes of fixed exchange rate regimes and high-amplitude fluctuations outcomes of more flexible exchange rate regimes? Is the duration of cyclical adjustments a function of policy regimes? Do **rules-driven** policy frameworks lead to longer mean cyclical durations than **discretion-driven frameworks**? Do the shifting price/output fluctuations reflect the likelihood that monetary policy is more discretionary in some periods (such as the inter-war era) than in others (such as the **Bretton Woods** era)?

A long-run historical perspective is particularly helpful for evaluating the relevance of long economic cycles. Chapter 3 examines two long cycle perspectives that have been developed to understand the past: **Kondratieff waves** of 50-year cycles and **Kuznets swings** of 20 years. Like other business cycle features, these patterns of fluctuation have not been stable over time. For example, while Kuznets swings had a pervasive influence on a large number of countries before 1914, the historical business cycle literature speaks of 'the passing of the Kuznets swing' after 1914 (Abramovitz, 1968). That new cyclical features emerged after 1914 is not in doubt. However, insights from this earlier period may help us to understand the cyclical implications of current institutional changes. For example, as the European economies attempt to create a monetary union, the homologies of the present institutional developments with the classical gold standard need to be considered. Chapter 3 argues that long fluctuations within the European bloc may re-emerge, with the gold standard era providing some interesting insights into the cyclical paths we expect to see in a changing world.

Bibliography

Abramovitz, M. (1968) 'The Passing of the Kuznets Cycle', *Economica*, 35, 349–67.

Bronfenbrenner, M. (1969) *Is the Business Cycle Obsolete?*, New York.

Chapter 2

Business cycles since 1870

Introduction

Fluctuations in economic activity are a feature of all modern economies. Although economic historians have documented the existence of cyclical movements before modern industrialisation, this chapter focuses on the period since 1870. After this date annual macroeconomic data are more reliable, allowing us to make quantitative comparisons over time and across countries. The evidence is considered across three historical periods: 1870–1913, 1919–38 and 1950–92. These three phases allow us to describe the evolution of cyclical processes and illustrate a number of important structural, institutional and policy features that condition the nature of economic cycles.

The period 1870–1913 represents the era of the classical gold standard. From 1879 to 1913 all of the four major industrial countries (Britain, France, Germany, and the US) were on a fixed exchange rate regime, with their respective currencies pegged to gold at a fixed rate. It is widely accepted that this institution had important implications for the conduct of national economic policy, greatly limiting the scope for discretionary monetary and fiscal policies. The structure of economies was also quite different in this era relative to more recent periods, in a number of ways. First, most international trade was **core–periphery** (north–south) **trade,** representing an exchange of primary commodities for manufactured goods that created linkages between economies with very different production structures. Secondly, the degree of international mobility of capital and labour was exceptionally high, creating the possibility of significant adjustment to shocks. Thirdly, the size of the agricultural sector, as a percentage of the total labour force and gross domestic product, was larger, increasing the impact of supply-side weather shocks on economies.

The inter-war era witnessed major discontinuities with the past. The gold standard gave way to a period of flexible exchange rates between 1919 and 1925; this was replaced by a distorted and maladjusted **gold exchange standard** in the mid-1920s which, in turn, collapsed with a series of discretionary and uncoordinated exchange rate changes in the 1930s (Eichengreen, 1992; Temin, 1989). Two other major developments affected business cycle behaviour: first, the transition from British to American leadership of the world economy, which has been seen to be of central importance for the international transmission of shocks (Kindleberger, 1983); secondly, the restriction of international migration flows to the New World and the collapse of international capital markets between 1928 and 1938, which symbolised the end of some of the stabilising adjustment mechanisms existing in the world economy before 1914.

The lessons of the inter-war experience led policy makers to seek stability in international exchange rates in the post-war period. The Bretton Woods arrangements linked exchange rates to the dollar with the **adjustable peg** mechanism. This system collapsed in the early 1970s and attempts were made to re-establish exchange rate stability within newly emerging trading blocs during the 1980s and 1990s. Comparing the post-war 'golden age' with the post-1973 era allows us to evaluate the effect of different policy regimes on business cycle behaviour. The post-war period is also interesting in the light of two important long-run structural changes. First, the rapid growth of the government sector in most of the major industrial countries has been noted as a stabilising influence on aggregate demand, reducing the volatility of business cycle fluctuations relative to the past (Tobin, 1980; Zarnowitz, 1992). Secondly, the rapid growth of intra-regional and **intra-industry trade** has resulted in significant changes to the structure of world trade, and thus in the international transmission of shocks.

This long-run historical perspective is in marked contrast to much recent work on business cycles that has sought to explain the stylised facts of post-war business cycles as if they were historically universal. Theories of business cycles need to explain both the stylised facts of particular epochs and the changes that are so marked across different periods. Only by understanding how business cycle behaviour is influenced by behavioural, institutional, structural and policy changes can we hope to understand business cycle behaviour in the future. To seek stylised facts that are stable over time and space is methodologically inconsistent with historical processes of economic change and empirically inconsistent with the evidence. One *conditional* prediction which is clear from previous patterns of behaviour is that it is unlikely that business cycles will have the same features in the decades to come as have been observed in the post-war era to date.

Explanatory frameworks

The causal frameworks for business cycles can be placed into two broad categories – the *propagation* and *impulse* perspectives

(Adelman, 1960). The former perceives cycles as arising from the endogenous workings of the economic system. For example, certain parameters of multiplier-accelerator models can generate endogenously recurring cycles. The impulse perspective views cycles as arising from the impact of exogenous shocks to the economy. Moreover, even random shocks are capable of generating economic cycles because shocks impose an adjustment path on the economic system (Lucas, 1981; Slutsky, 1937). These two approaches to business cycles are not mutually exclusive. For example, a propagation mechanism is needed to convert random shocks into business cycles. Similarly, economists who emphasise the propagation perspective recognise that shocks determine the specific historical details of particular cycles and, thus, can account for why it is that one cycle may be longer than another or why one depression is more severe than another. Partly because of this interaction of causal frameworks, it has proved extremely difficult to decide whether economic cycles are best understood by emphasising propagation or impulse frameworks.

The classical gold standard era

Describing business cycles

Describing the cyclical path of economies during the period 1870–1913 is not a simple exercise. Research on business cycles has often been undertaken with the assumption that any annual economic variable can be decomposed into three separable parts: trend, cycle and random influences. Within this perspective *the cycle* can be identified by fitting a simple long-run trend to the data and then taking the pattern of deviations about this trend to describe cyclical fluctuations.

Two problems need to be considered when seeking to describe the cyclical path: first, in the pre-1914 period a number of cycles, with differing periods and amplitudes, coexisted; secondly, an important assumption that needs to hold to make such a decomposition valid is that economies follow **trend-stationary paths**, which means that economic growth takes place around a steady trend. Accepting this assumption, when it is false, will lead to serious errors of interpretation: trend variations will wrongly be depicted as cyclical variations. The assumption of a steady trend has been rejected from analysis of twentieth-century macroeconomic data (Nelson and Plosser, 1982).[1] However, for the pre-1914 gold standard period, tests of trend-stationarity have yielded mixed results.

At the aggregate level of observation, the path of gross domestic product (GDP) in some of the leading industrial countries followed trend-stationary paths for much of the pre-1914 gold standard period (Crafts *et al.*, 1989; Mills, 1991; Perron and Phillips, 1987). This is the case for Britain and the US over 1870–1913. In contrast, the French and German GDP trends can best be depicted as a **random walk** or a segmented trend.

To allow for both these problems we employ the Kalman filter time-series estimation method of Koopman *et al.* (1995); this provides a statistical technique for decomposing the cyclical paths (the data can have up to three cycles) from the long-run trend, which can be either stationary or stochastic

---

1 Recent studies have drawn a distinction between *segmented trends* and *random walks* (Perron, 1989). The idea of segmented trends recognises that a few large shocks and policy regime changes have shifted the long-run path of economies; the random walk perspective rejects any well defined trend periods.

(the methodology of the Kalman filter is described in the appendix to this chapter). In general there will be a number of models that describe the data; the models reported are ones that have been derived from testing more general specifications and that yield good fits.

The cyclical decomposition of British GDP is displayed in Figure 1. Beginning with the most general model, the British case suggests the existence of two stochastic cycles, of 8.6 years and 24.6 years. If we impose only one cycle on the data we find a stochastic cycle of 12.3 years. The US economy displays a deterministic short cycle of approximately 5 years and a **long swing** of 19.2 years (Figure 2). There is also evidence of a stochastic cycle of 10.8 years. The German economy displays a stochastic short cycle of 10.8 years and a stochastic long cycle of 23.8 years (Figure 3). French GDP can be decomposed into a deterministic short cycle of 4.5 years, a stochastic cycle of 7.7 years and a deterministic long cycle of 20 years (Figure 4). The general pattern that emerges from this exercise is that a multiplicity of cycles was the norm in the pre-1914 economies.

A more complete description of pre-1914 cycles also needs to note that the path of GDP is the outcome of very different movements in more disaggregated component series. Many key economic time-series in the pre-1914 era follow random walks, including exports, investment and consumption (Catao and Solomou, 1993; Solomou and Catao, 1994). Macroeconomic trend-stationarity, as reflected in the path of GDP in some of the major countries, is the outcome of equilibrium adjustment to shocks affecting these component series. This perspective is similar to that put forward by Matthews (1959), who argued that the short trade cycle was the *outcome* of inverse Kuznets swings in home and overseas investment, which were correlated with inverse swings in investment and exports:

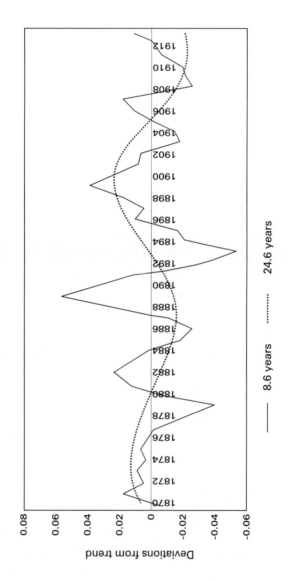

Figure 1 Kalman filter decomposition of British GDP cycles, 1870–1913.

8.6 years ·········· 24.6 years

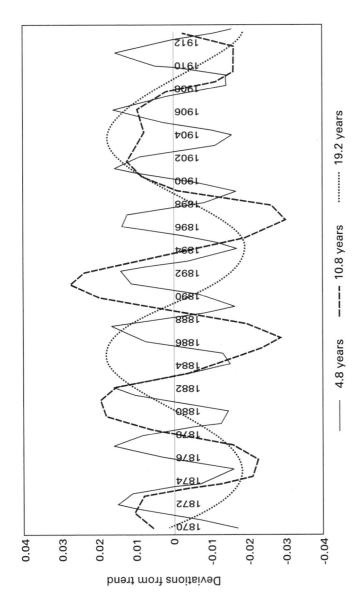

Figure 2 Kalman filter decomposition of US GDP cycles, 1870–1913.

— 4.8 years   - - - 10.8 years   ······· 19.2 years

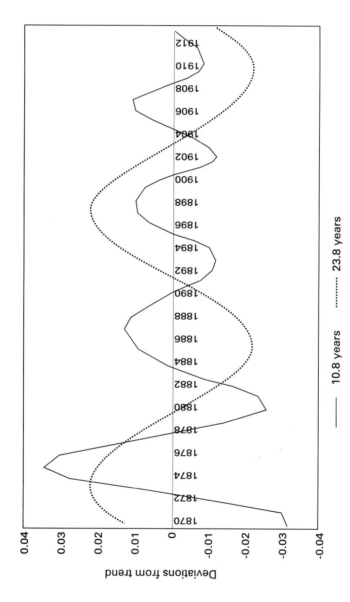

Figure 3 Kalman filter decomposition of German GDP cycles, 1870–1913.

—— 10.8 years ⋯⋯ 23.8 years

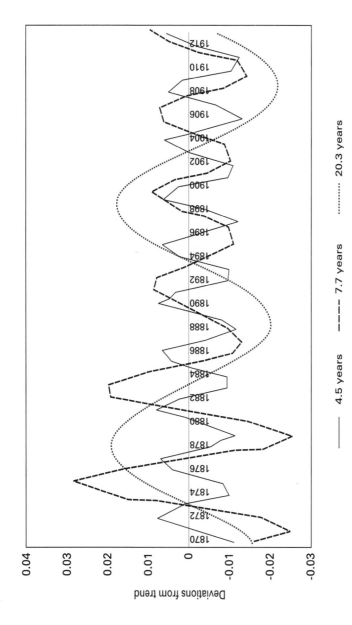

Figure 4 Kalman filter decomposition of French GDP cycles, 1870–1913.

——— 4.5 years ——— 7.7 years ‧‧‧‧‧‧ 20.3 years

It appears therefore – and this is the important conclusion – that the seven- to ten-year periodicity of fluctuations in national income derived mainly from the existence of two unsynchronised waves, each of roughly twice that duration, in home and foreign investment respectively, rather than from the existence of a seven- to ten-year cycle in either taken by itself. (Matthews, 1959, p. 220)

The adjustment mechanisms operating during the gold standard period that generated these outcomes are considered further below.

Rules-driven policy frameworks and business cycles

The trend-stationarity of the macroeconomic growth process of some of the major industrial countries during the classical gold standard era stands in marked contrast to the random walk path of the twentieth century. Crafts and Mills (1992) suggest that this may reflect the impact of a rules-driven policy framework (such as the gold standard) in stabilising the underlying growth path of economies. In contrast, the discretionary policy rules of the twentieth century have allowed economies to deviate randomly and persistently away from their long-run supply-side growth paths. The volatility of the main industrial economies was also significantly lower during the gold standard period relative to the inter-war era (Sheffrin, 1988).

Given the importance of macroeconomic institutions in influencing the cyclical process, this idea warrants further evaluation. In order to understand how macroeconomic trend-stationarity arises, we need to consider the type of adjustment mechanisms operating during this period. Figure 5 presents a stylised description of a number of adjustment processes observed during this period. Three aspects of the pre-1914

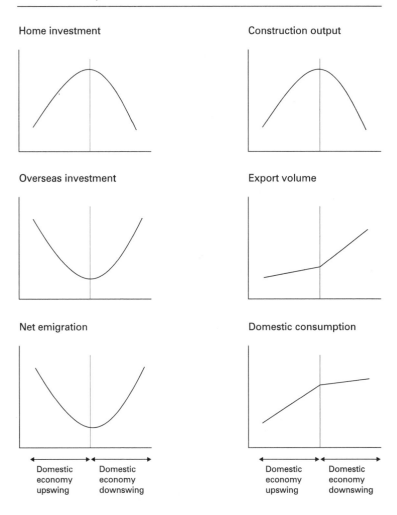

Figure 5 A stylised view of long-swing adjustments.

world economy are of central importance to generating adjustment to shocks: first, international labour mobility was exceptionally high; secondly, capital mobility from the industrial countries (Britain, France and Germany) to the newly industrialising and **primary producing countries** created liquidity in the international economy; thirdly, capital flows sustained aggregate demand (by stimulating exports) during episodes of depression in the capital-exporting countries. These features resulted in stabilising interactions between the domestic economy and the international economy.[2] For example, depressed conditions in the national economy gave rise to a cyclical propagation mechanism that resulted in an adjustment of the labour market via overseas migration. In the case of Britain and Germany, depressed home investment opportunities were associated with rising emigration; in the case of France and the US, depressed home investment opportunities resulted in a marked contraction of immigration. The fall in home investment was also correlated with a rise of overseas investment and the income transfer overseas created demand for the exports of industrial countries. Thus, compensatory equilibrating mechanisms were operating in the pre-1914 era. A rules-driven policy framework *by itself* could not be expected to generate these cyclical outcomes. It is the combination of historically unique circumstances with the gold standard policy framework that provided stabilising adjustment paths. Such a conclusion raises strong doubts as to the stabilising effect of the gold standard policy regime in itself. Bayoumi and Eichengreen (1996) provide empirical evidence to support this conclusion: they find that the relative stability of the gold standard epoch cannot be explained by an absence of destabilising shocks; instead, they show that it was the rapid adjustments to disturbances which resulted in relative macroeconomic stability.

2   The limited extent of democracy during this period also constrained working-class influence on the national political agenda, creating a more stable political environment for the policy regime.

International economic cycles?

One business cycle stylised fact that has been discussed in the recent literature is that the timing of business cycle fluctuations differed significantly across the major industrial countries[3] (Backus and Kehoe, 1992; Eichengreen, 1994). At face value this suggests that nation-specific shocks were more important than international business cycle transmission mechanisms. Table 1 shows that the only statistically significant correlation between different national GDP cycles is that between Germany and the US, and that is small. The robustness of this result can be questioned on technical grounds. The result is dependent on the kind of filter being used to decompose economic cycles. Backus and Kehoe use the **Hodrick–Prescott (H–P) filter**, which can be criticised for generating artefact cycles from the data (Cogley and Nason, 1995; Harvey and Jaeger, 1993). Moreover, the H–P filter focuses on deriving one short cycle from the data when, in fact, the pre-1914 data verify the existence of a number of cycles. The relevant question that needs to be addressed is whether countries shared common cyclical paths at particular cyclical frequencies. To illustrate the importance of this point, consider

3   In order to describe pre-1914 business cycles we have to make use of macroeconomic data, the reliability of which is much less than that of comparable data for the post-war period (Catao and Solomou, 1993; Solomou, 1987; Solomou and Weale, 1991). As a result there are serious problems of comparability of macroeconomic data which have been constructed using very different national accounting methods. These are not easily resolved and we should be aware that some of the results of the literature on business cycles are dependent on making international comparisons from these data sources: this means that the conclusions for this period have to be seen in the context of large measurement errors.

Table 1   International output correlations: pre-war

	Britain	US	Germany	Japan
Britain	–			
US	0.01	–		
	(0.14)			
Germany	0.03	-0.40	–	
	(0.12)	(0.13)*		
Japan	0.08	-0.22	-0.14	–
	(0.17)	(0.15)	(0.17)	

Source: Backus and Kehoe (1992, p. 876).
The entries show the contemporaneous correlations of cyclical variations
of output. Numbers in parentheses are standard errors: only the German–
American correlation is significantly different from zero.
*Significant at the 5 per cent level.

whether Britain and the US shared common cycles over this
period. Estimating a two-cycle multivariate Kalman filter
model for US and British GDP suggests that the two economies
shared a common stochastic cycle of 9.9 years (with a cross-
correlation of 0.47) and a deterministic long cycle of 23.7 years
which was inverse across the two economies. The two economies were highly integrated, confirming the historical accounts
of an 'Atlantic economy' (Thomas, 1954).

The degree of integration of the international economy
during the gold standard era was reflected in the existence of
the type of international adjustments we have discussed above.
Depressed investment and consumption opportunities in industrial countries were reflected in rising overseas investment,
migration flows and a stimulus of the export sectors. This is an
era when the long swing cyclical process was so pervasive
across countries that it does not make sense to analyse business

cycles as short fluctuations in GDP. The evidence reported above suggests that a multiplicity of cycles was the norm in the pre-1914 epoch. There is enough evidence to suggest that we can reject the idea that pre-1914 cycles were nation specific, although more research is needed to document the cyclical linkages across countries during this period.

Business cycle impulses

Export shocks

Export shocks have been seen as a key variable accounting for macroeconomic fluctuations over 1870–1913 (Ford, 1981; Hatton, 1990). The path of exports from *all* the major industrial countries followed random walks during the gold standard period (Solomou and Catao, 1994), suggesting that shocks to exports need to be linked to business cycles via the adjustment processes existing in this era.[4]

What determined the path of exports during this period? Solomou and Catao (1994) model the movements of exports from the leading industrial countries during the gold standard era as sharing common trends with the real **effective exchange rate** and the path of world trade. Although the core industrial countries sustained fixed exchange rates with each other during this period, much trade was conducted as core–periphery (north–south) trade. The periphery was unable to sustain a fixed exchange rate for much of the pre-1914 era. Thus, although the nominal exchange rates of the core industrial

4 In technical terms, because exports follow a random walk while GDP follows a trend-stationary path, the cyclical effect of exports needs to be analysed via linkages with other, non-stationary series, such as home and overseas investment.

countries were fixed relative to gold, their effective exchange rates (weighted with a basket of currencies of all their trading partners) showed marked trend and short-term variations. Real effective exchange rates were also influenced by changes in a number of economic fundamentals. First, under conditions of differential productivity growth across countries and sectors, as was the case before 1914, real exchange rates will change in the medium and long term (Balassa, 1964). Secondly, in the case of creditor nations (Britain, France and Germany) that earned large net income flows from accumulated overseas assets, we would expect, *ceteris paribus*, an appreciation of real exchange rates (Maddison, 1982; Pollard, 1989; Rowthorn and Solomou, 1991). Thirdly, national tariff policies induce real exchange rate differences in the long run (Sommariva and Tullio, 1987). Given the uncoordinated nature of trade policies before 1914, this is expected to be a relevant factor during this period. In particular, Britain's unilateral free trade policy gave rise to long-run depreciation relative to the more protected industrial countries. The impact of nominal and price effects on the real effective exchange rate behaviour of the **core industrial countries** resulted in real effective exchange rates that transmitted significant shocks to trade (Solomou and Catao, 1994).

Weather shocks

Weather explanations of economic cycles go back a long way. As early as 1847, Hyde Clarke offered an explanation for 10–11-year economic cycles and a 54-year cycle in terms of astronomical and meteorological variations. Later in the nineteenth century Jevons (1884, p. 235) argued:

> after some further careful inquiry, I am perfectly convinced that these decennial crises do depend upon meteorological

variations of like period, which again depend, in all probability, upon cosmical variations of which we have evidence in the frequency of sun-spot, auroras, and magnetic perturbations.

Modern economists have tended to dismiss these ideas as simplistic. Economic historians have made similar assumptions: for example, Aldcroft and Fearon (1972) concluded that harvest fluctuations were not important to business cycle behaviour after the mid-nineteenth century. Such generalisations are misleading. The agricultural sector accounted for a large proportion of the output and investment fluctuations of the British economy during the late nineteenth century (Feinstein *et al.*, 1982; Solomou, 1987, 1994). Weather effects on agricultural production cannot be ruled out on *a priori* grounds. Weather effects will also be important to other highly cyclical sectors, such as construction. In this section, instead of dismissing the impact of weather by assumption, I will report the results of empirical analysis relating to agriculture and construction.

Using semi-parametric statistical methods to quantify the adverse effects of weather shocks on agricultural output, Khatri and Solomou (1996) found that weather shocks were central to the fluctuations observed in agricultural production over 1867–1913. The weather effects were non-linear (with conditions of drought and excessive moisture both having adverse effects) and asymmetric (with conditions of excessive moisture having larger impacts than conditions of drought). During 1867–1913, the adverse effects were as high as 10–13 per cent of mean production levels for conditions of excess moisture (such as the 1870s); conditions of relative drought (such as the 1890s) reduced output by only 2–3 per cent of mean production levels.

Showing that agriculture remained a weather-sensitive sector in this period is not sufficient evidence to argue that the
agro-climatic relationship was important in its impact on
aggregate fluctuations. The extreme weather conditions of the
1870s reduced aggregate agricultural production by approximately 10–13 per cent. The sector accounted for about 15 per
cent of GDP in the 1870s, yielding a supply-side shock between
approximately 1.5 per cent of GDP (0.15×0.1) and 1.95 per
cent (0.15×0.13).[5] As weather conditions returned to more
normal conditions in the 1880s, the effect on GDP was favourable. In order to gain a perspective on the size of these shocks
we should note that business cycle fluctuations generated GDP
deviations of about 4 per cent from trend values (see Figure 1),
suggesting that weather shocks can account for approximately
one-third of aggregate fluctuations during this period.

During the 1890s the weather shocks affecting the agricultural sector were quite different: low rainfall and high mean
temperatures gave rise to a cluster of relative drought conditions.
The macroeconomic effects of these shocks were of less
importance. The negative effect of drought conditions averaged
2 per cent of aggregate agricultural production (Khatri and
Solomou, 1996). Given that the size of the agricultural sector
had declined to about 7 per cent of GDP by the 1890s, this
implies a supply-side shock of 0.14 per cent of GDP ($0.02 \times
0.07$). This marked shift in the effect of weather shocks reflects

5 Although the 1870s saw an increase in imports of agricultural
   commodities relative to domestic agricultural output, during 1873–81
   the sectoral terms of trade were moving in favour of agriculture and
   international terms of trade were moving against Britain. Thus,
   imports of food and domestic food supplies were being purchased at a
   rising relative cost, suggesting adverse supply-side shocks on the
   sector.

both the different nature of weather conditions in the 1890s and the structural shift in British agriculture away from arable to pasture production, which is less sensitive to weather conditions. The evidence suggests that supply-side weather shocks were still very important to the fluctuations of agricultural production during 1870–1913. Given the relatively small agricultural sector in Britain by the end of the nineteenth century, the impact of weather is expected to be significantly larger on the Continental European economies: in 1870, the agricultural sectors in France and Germany accounted for over 40 per cent of GDP. Given the sectoral structure of economies during this period, the evidence suggests that supply-side shocks arising from weather variations were still a very important influence on aggregate fluctuations. Economists and economic historians need to re-evaluate the role of weather in business cycle fluctuations.

Construction is also recognised as a highly weather-sensitive sector, since building work is mainly undertaken on open sites (Jones, 1964; Maunder, 1986; Prior, 1989; Russo, 1966). During the nineteenth century almost the whole annual production of bricks took place between April and September, when weather conditions were favourable (Jones, 1964).

Solomou and Wu (1998) used a semi-parametric statistical method to estimate the effects of weather shocks on the construction sector growth rate.[6] Annual average temperature had a non-linear effect on production. The effect of annual total rainfall was linear and negatively correlated with the growth of construction output. The effect range was quite wide and weather

---

6 Construction sector output was non-trend-stationary during this period; hence the modelling is focused on the growth rate, which is stationary.

variables accounted for approximately 20 per cent of the total variation of the annual construction growth over the period. The evidence thus suggests that exogenous weather shocks also had a significant impact on the growth rate of construction output. The non-linear nature of the relationship implies that the magnitude of the effect was a function of the specific combination of weather shocks in a particular year. Solomou and Wu (1998) derived the magnitude of the effect of weather shocks on GDP using a national accounting analysis, whereby the annual weather effect on construction was weighted by the share of the sector in GDP. The aggregate effect for the period 1862–1913 ranged from –0.35 per cent to 0.15 per cent of GDP growth. Comparing the weather effects on the construction sector with those for agriculture suggests that before 1890 the main impact of weather shocks on the macroeconomy arose from agro-climatic linkages.[7]

Technological shocks
The importance of technological shocks to business cycle discussions has been emphasised in the modern literature on **real business cycle shocks**. For example, Kydland and Prescott (1982) assume that economic fluctuations result from uncertainty in the rate of technological change. Documenting these supply-side technology shocks has, however, proved difficult. Bayoumi and Eichengreen (1996) used the time-series technique of a restricted **vector autoregression** (VAR) to measure the magnitude of aggregate supply and aggregate demand shocks. In a study of the US, Britain, Germany, Italy, Australia,

---

7   The pattern of co-variation between the two sectoral weather effects is near zero, suggesting that the two effects were independent of each other.

Sweden and Denmark during the period 1880–1913 they found that the magnitudes of supply and demand shocks were approximately equal. However, establishing that supply-side shocks were important is not sufficient to distinguish technological from other supply-side shocks. For example, as noted above, weather shocks were also a very important supply-side shock during this period.

The real business cycle literature has employed the Solow **total factor productivity** (TFP) residual to identify and measure the size of technological shocks (Plosser, 1989). However, this has been shown to be inadequate in that movements in the TFP residual are unable to distinguish technological from demand shocks (Mankiw, 1989). Matthews *et al.* (1982) showed that during 1856–1913 TFP variations closely followed GDP variations, suggesting an important role for demand effects on TFP variations.

Crafts and Mills (1992) provide an historical application of the real business cycle perspective to the British economy during the period 1850–1913. The real business cycle approach is significantly qualified on two major counts: first, it fails to explain investment behaviour; secondly, it cannot account for the observed real wage fluctuations. It seems safe to conclude that although technology shocks are expected to be important to business cycles, explanations that neglect demand-side and other supply-side shocks provide an incomplete picture of the cyclical process during this period. Such an evaluation should not be interpreted as a dismissal of the relevance of technological shocks; however, far more research is needed to identify technological and other innovational shocks. Given the importance of technical progress to long-run growth, it is likely that shocks to technology will have cyclical effects. Considering the results of Bayoumi and Eichengreen

(1996), which suggest that supply and demand shocks were of equal importance, with the evidence which suggests that weather shocks have an important supply-side effect on aggregate fluctuations during this period, gives us some idea about the relative importance of technological shocks.

Monetary shocks

The idea that (unanticipated) monetary shocks can generate real economic fluctuations has been emphasised in the rational expectations literature (Barro, 1981; Lucas, 1975, 1977). The basic theoretical idea is that random monetary shocks create 'noise' in the economic system, which acts to fool rational agents, changing their behaviour with respect to choices over work and leisure and consumption and investment.

Although misperception models of business cycles were influential in the 1970s, it is now recognised that their ability to explain business cycle behaviour in the post-war period has proved extremely weak (Gordon, 1986; Kydland and Prescott, 1982). What role do monetary variations play in the gold standard era? The existing historical literature provides us with mixed results: Aldcroft and Fearon (1972) examined the British evidence and concluded that the influence of monetary factors varied from cycle to cycle, making it difficult to draw general conclusions; Ford (1981) argued that money supply accommodated itself to changes in real activity rather than causing it; Friedman and Schwartz (1982) concluded that British money supply variations did not influence *real* output. In contrast, Eichengreen (1983) found that during 1870–1914 'fluctuations in the monetary base emerge as the single most significant determinant of the trade cycle'. However, using more recent money supply data and improved trend-elimination methods Capie and Mills (1991) found that monetary shocks do not *cause* macroeconomic fluctuations in a **Granger causality** sense.

In contrast, studies of the US show a clear influence of monetary shocks on real variables. Friedman and Schwartz (1982) and Capie and Mills (1992) both found that monetary shocks influenced US output fluctuations. Major monetary shocks led to financial crises, entailing banking collapses and a rapid contraction of the money supply in the downturns beginning in 1873, 1893 and 1907, which had significant contractionary cyclical effects on real output.

The monetary and macroeconomic data for other countries do not allow us to generalise these findings. However, the comparison of the US and Britain does suggest that being on the gold standard was not *sufficient* to eliminate the importance of monetary shocks in business cycle fluctuations. The structure of domestic financial institutions is an additional factor in accounting for the observed differences in the nature and magnitude of monetary shocks.

Conclusions: gold standard

- The institution of the gold standard is not sufficient to account for the relative cyclical stability of this period. Shocks were as large as for other periods: what was different was the ability of economies to adjust to shocks. International adjustment mechanisms, via exports, migration and overseas investment, were particularly strong.
- The low co-variation of national business cycles observed in some of the recent literature seems to be an artefact of statistical methodology. Only if we choose to *define* business cycles arbitrarily as a unique short cycle of GDP does the result have any meaning. The cyclical process of the

period entailed the existence of longer-duration cyclical adjustment mechanisms. Unless this feature is integrated into the analysis there is the risk of generating statistical artefacts.

- The conventional perspective on pre-1914 business cycles depicts the existence of a regular nine-year macroeconomic cycle, often referred to as the **trade cycle**; the evidence considered rejects the existence of a *regular* nine-year cycle. Long swings and shorter macroeconomic fluctuations co-existed and interacted with each other. This feature has important implications when thinking about the robustness of some of the recent empirical findings. For example, if the monetary–output link is found to be weak at a particular cyclical frequency, this should not be interpreted as a rejection of all monetary effects on economic cycles.

- The structure of pre-1914 economies implies that agricultural fluctuations, significantly determined by weather shocks, were still an important supply-side influence on the cyclical path of the macroeconomy. Weather also affected other weather-sensitive activities, such as construction, although the macroeconomic aspect of this effect is relatively small when compared with that of the agricultural sector.

- Supply-side shocks and demand-side shocks were of similar importance over this period. Further research is needed to decompose supply-side shocks into technological shocks, weather shocks and shocks to consumer taste. Similarly, demand-side shocks need to be further broken up into monetary shocks (for example, gold discoveries or interest rate changes) and international nominal exchange rate variations arising from the policy stance of countries outside the gold standard.

The inter-war era

During 1919–38, the world economy witnessed economic fluctuations that were, in many ways, distinctly different from those of the past. As noted above, while business cycles are a recurrent phenomenon their characteristics evolve. The following are some of the more important changes that emerged in the inter-war period:

- *Macroeconomic trend-stationarity.* During the pre-1914 gold standard era, at least some of the major industrial countries displayed trend-stationarity in their aggregate growth paths, with a tendency to grow along a stable path in the long run. This is the case for Britain and the US over 1870–1913 and for Germany during 1880–1913. During the inter-war era, these underlying growth paths were displaced in a persistently downward direction as a result of adverse business cycle shocks during the early 1920s and early 1930s. The timing of these adverse shocks varied by country: for example, Germany and Britain experienced persistent adverse effects in the early 1920s while the US saw persistent adverse shocks in the early 1930s.
- *The passing of the Kuznets swing.* The pre-1914 economies witnessed Kuznets swings in the trends of a number of important variables, including GDP, migration, agricultural production, construction output, domestic and overseas investment, consumption, exports and the balance of trade. During the inter-war period shorter cycles in all these variables became the norm, suggesting a break in the long-swing growth process (Abramovitz, 1968).
- *Business cycle amplitudes.* Business cycle volatility was significantly higher in the inter-war than in the pre-1914 era

(Backus and Kehoe, 1992; Sheffrin, 1988). Table 2 presents
data that allow us to compare the variance of the inter-war
period with the post-war and pre-1914 periods: the variance of GDP and industrial production during the inter-war
period is historically unique.

Table 2 Standard deviation measures (percentages) of output
volatility (standard errors in parenthesis)

Country	Pre-war	Inter-war	Post-war
Australia	6.30	4.85	1.93
	(0.72)	(0.75)	(0.19)
Britain	2.12	3.47	1.62
	(0.24)	(0.37)	(0.21)
Canada	4.47	9.80	2.22
	(0.43)	(1.40)	(0.23)
Denmark	3.02	3.41	1.88
	(0.22)	(0.64)	(0.20)
Germany	3.35	10.19	2.30
	(0.32)	(1.61)	(0.28)
Italy	2.52	3.59	2.05
	(0.24)	(0.46)	(0.17)
Japan	2.42	3.13	3.11
	(0.24)	(0.44)	(0.32)
Norway	1.85	3.49	1.76
	(0.16)	(0.65)	(0.17)
Sweden	2.43	3.74	1.45
	(0.37)	(0.59)	(0.12)
US	4.28	9.33	2.26
	(0.38)	(1.27)	(0.18)

Source: Backus and Kehoe (1992, p. 871).

Table 3 International output correlations: inter-war

	Britain	US	Germany	Japan
Britain	–			
US	0.74 (0.11)*	–		
Germany	0.89 (0.05)*	0.78 (0.08)*	–	
Japan	0.25 (0.24)	-0.05 (0.24)	0.58 (0.20)*	–

Source: Backus and Kehoe (1992, p. 876).
The entries show the contemporaneous correlations of cyclical variations of output. Numbers in parenthesis are standard errors.
*Significant at the 5 per cent level.

- *International cycles.* Business cycles showed high levels of international co-movement in the inter-war era (Table 3). Table 4 shows that this high level of international co-movements stands out even when comparisons are made with the post-war era.

These new features raise a number of important questions. First, is the persistence of shocks influenced by the collapse of the rules-driven policy framework of the pre-1914 gold standard, and its replacement by more discretionary policy frameworks in the 1920s and 1930s? Secondly, why did the international adjustments of the long-swing process (such as the inverse home and overseas investment swings) come to an end during the inter-war period, and what implications did this have for the stability of the world economy? Thirdly, is the

Table 4   International output correlations: post-war

	Britain	US	Germany	Japan	Canada
Britain	–				
US	0.48	–			
	(0.13)*				
Germany	0.40	0.18	–		
	(0.12)*	(0.20)			
Japan	0.24	0.51	0.21	–	
	(0.16)	(0.13)*	(0.18)		
Canada	0.36	0.64	0.07	0.18	–
	(0.15)*	(0.09)*	(0.17)	(0.13)	

Source: Backus and Kehoe (1992, p. 876).
The entries show the contemporaneous correlations of cyclical variations
of output. Numbers in parenthesis are standard errors.
*Significant at the 5 per cent level.

increased amplitude of inter-war business cycles the outcome of
new institutional features, such as increased wage rigidity?
Finally, did these new features have implications for the causal
processes determining business cycle behaviour during 1919–
38 compared with the gold standard era?

Before we consider some of these analytical issues it would
be useful to present an overview of the major economic
fluctuations influencing the leading industrial countries over
this period. Given the short period involved, this descriptive
overview will provide the context for discussing some of the
broader questions raised in this section. Econometric analysis
of inter-war business cycles is constrained by the limited
degrees of freedom implied by such a short period.

Overview

1920–1 depression

The year 1920–1 was one of depression in all the major industrial countries that attempted to bring to an end post-war inflation, including Britain, France and the US. For Britain this was the most severe slump experienced this century, being more severe in its effects than the world depression of 1929–32. In order to understand the depression forces of 1920–1 we have to consider the inflationary path of the immediate post-war period. Post-war reconstruction generated both demand-pull and cost-push inflationary pressures. Between 1918 and 1920, the economy operated at full employment, with a rapid growth of demand for consumer and investment goods at home and abroad: this generated demand-pull inflationary pressures. Cost-push pressures were also present. Dowie (1975) emphasised the importance of the introduction of the eight-hour day in 1919 as a major inflationary force: weekly working hours fell from 50 to 43.5, amounting to a 13 per cent fall. The fall occurred without a reduction in weekly wages, which meant that real wages for a normal week rose by the full amount of the reduction in hours. The combined effects of demand and cost pressures on the British inflation rate caused it to rise faster than the US rate. At the same time, in November 1919, the British government announced the official policy intention of returning to the gold standard at the pre-1914 gold parity. Since a differential had arisen between British and US inflation rates between 1914 and 1919 the government was clearly announcing a forthcoming contractionary monetary policy. Given the system of flexible exchange rates that was introduced in 1919, the effect of the restrictive monetary policy announcement was to result in an 'overshooting' of the real effective exchange rate (Broadberry, 1986). The restrictive monetary policy also led consumers to hold to inelastic inflationary expectations, reducing consumption and increasing money demand. This analysis implies that the rise in interest rates in April 1920 was not the impulse that pushed the economy into depression but a symbol that recessionary forces were well under way from late 1919, resulting from the deflationary monetary policy announcements and the wage gap in the labour market.

One of the outstanding features of the depression of 1921 is the exceptionally large fall in British exports – 30 per cent. However, the export collapse cannot be seen as an *exogenous* shock: under flexible exchange rates, the contractionary monetary policy and the supply-side changes in the labour market resulted in an appreciation of the real exchange rate, leading to a large fall in exports. Thus, the collapse of exports, though important for understanding the dynamics of the depression, was not the *cause* in a simple exogenous sense.

The severity of the British depression was unmatched by that of any other country. Both the US and France saw milder depressions (Patat and Luttala, 1990; Romer, 1988): while British GDP fell by 10 per cent (Solomou and Weale, 1996), US GDP fell by 2.4 per cent (Romer, 1988) and French GDP by only 1.6 per cent (Maddison, 1991). The major difference in these relative experiences is to be found in different exchange rate policies and supply-side conditions. Britain's commitment to an early return to the gold standard at the pre-1914 parity resulted in a rapid appreciation of the real exchange rate during 1919–22 that had serious adverse output effects. In the case of France, there was a more gradualist approach to returning to the stability of the pre-1914 gold standard and the strong competitive position of the US allowed it to return to the gold standard as early as 1919. These different exchange rate policies meant that monetary deflation was far more severe in Britain than in the other major industrial countries; when combined with the adverse supply-side shift induced by the fall in hours of work in 1919, the British economy was faced with a very severe contraction. In contrast, Romer (1988) has noted the importance of favourable supply-side shifts in the US economy, induced by the collapse of production costs in 1920–1.[8]

The case of Germany further illustrates the importance of monetary policy during 1920–1. In the same year German GDP grew by over 10 per cent and exports by 21 per cent, despite stagnation in world income growth (Maddison, 1991). This is explained by a significantly depreciated exchange rate. The rapid depreciation of the nominal exchange rate resulted in a real depreciation that gave a large stimulus to exports; at the same time, high inflation reduced real wages with favourable supply-side effects on profitability and investment (Sommariva and Tullio, 1987). Depression in the leading capital suppliers also meant that there was an excess supply of liquidity in the world economy, some of which found its way as capital imports in the German economy as investors were speculating on a Reichmark appreciation (Holtfrerich, 1986).

Economic recovery, 1921–9

Economic recovery during the 1920s was conditioned by exchange rate policies. During the 1920s the world economy witnessed a variety of exchange rate regimes. The US remained on the gold standard throughout 1919–33; some countries

---

8 A bumper harvest in 1921 gave a favourable supply-side shock to the US economy. The agricultural sector accounted for over 15 per cent of US GDP.

(such as Britain, Denmark, Norway and Sweden) left the gold standard during the war or the immediate post-war period, returning to the pre-1914 parity in the mid-1920s; Belgium, France and Italy returned to the gold standard in the 1920s but at a significantly depreciated exchange rate relative to the pre-1914 rate; others, such as Japan and Spain, allowed their currencies to float for longer, never returning to the gold standard in the 1920s. These cross-country differences in exchange rate policies allow us to evaluate their effect on cyclical recovery.

Exchange rate policies were also an important factor in the national recovery paths of the 1920s. In a comparative analysis of Britain and the Scandinavian economies, Broadberry (1984) argues that overvaluation of the currency caused poor cyclical economic performance, as measured by high unemployment rates. Eichengreen (1986, 1992), using a larger cross-section, of 12 countries, over 1921–7 (Britain, France, Norway, Sweden, Italy, Spain, Denmark, Holland, Canada, the US, Australia and Japan), found a significant correlation between changes in exchange rates and changes in industrial production. Eichengreen (1986) showed that, controlling for the magnitude of wartime disruption, countries that allowed their exchange rates to depreciate in the 1920s saw stronger cyclical recoveries than other countries.

Countries that returned to the gold standard at the 1913 parity also performed worse in the long run than the countries undergoing a currency depreciation: both Germany and Britain failed to return to their pre-1914 trend growth paths during the 1920s, while the US and France were relatively more successful at doing so (Solomou, 1996). The explanation for this adverse effect on economic growth is to be found in the persistent adverse effects of the cyclical shocks of the early post-war reconstruction period. Two mechanisms were central to this outcome.

First, in order to achieve the exchange rate target of the pre-1914 gold parity, governments had to pursue a contractionary monetary policy during the early 1920s. When the pre-war parity was re-established, often at an overvalued exchange rate, monetary policy had to be used to sustain the exchange rate target. High real and nominal interest rates persisted throughout the 1920s. Moreover, one of the pillars of the credibility of the gold standard was the policy of **balanced budgets**; hence, given contemporary economic ideology, the government would not expand the economy via the use of fiscal policy. High interest rates prevented the potential expansion of interest-sensitive sectors such as housing (Broadberry, 1986).

Secondly, the price deflation of countries returning to the gold standard at the pre-1914 parity was rapid. The full implication of this deflation on economic growth has to be linked to the immediate post-war boom. In the expectation of a prosperous future, with the anticipated weakening of Germany from international competition, the British staple export sectors (iron and steel, textiles, shipbuilding, coal) had increased their level of debt to finance much-needed investment. The rapid and *permanent* deflation of the early 1920s left these industries with a large real debt burden (Solomou, 1996). Given the government's commitment to the lower price level, new investment by existing firms was held back as they struggled to meet debt repayments under conditions of exceptionally high real interest rates.

The world depression, 1929–33
Two key features distinguish this depression from all previous depressions: first, it stands out as the most severe depression in

the world economy throughout the nineteenth and twentieth centuries; secondly, the depression was, to all intents and purposes, a *world* depression. These unique features make the Great Depression an outlier in the history of business cycles which has resulted in an abundance of theories to explain (and perhaps over-explain) the event.

Much of the early research focused on the causes of the US depression, in the belief that this offered the key to understanding the world depression. Temin (1976) argued that an unexplained collapse of consumer expenditure caused the depression: this is equivalent to arguing that 'animal spirits', determining shifts in consumer expectations, caused the depression. In contrast, Friedman and Schwartz (1963) argued that the contractionary monetary policy pursued by the US Federal Reserve (the FED) during 1928–33 caused the severe contraction. Given the size of the US economy, the collapse of 1929 was quickly transmitted to the world economy via a collapse of capital and trade flows in a fixed exchange rate regime.

More recent literature has questioned both strands of this approach. First, the type of shocks that were emphasised are inadequate to understand the severity of the depression. The idea that a large policy-induced collapse of the money supply caused the US depression is incomplete. Bernanke (1983) and Calomiris (1993) showed that the role of financial markets needs to be given careful consideration in addition to the simple monetary transmission mechanisms. Financial collapse generated supply-side shocks on economies, restricting the level of credit availability and raising the cost of credit. Olney (1991) showed that the legal/ institutional structure of credit that evolved in the 1920s gave rise to high consumption volatility during the Great

Depression.[9] Thus, what is an unexplained event in Temin's framework is now better understood.

Secondly, although the US depression is best accounted for as a nation-specific phenomenon,[10] it seems misleading to argue that the Great Depression was simply transmitted to the world economy from the shocks affecting the US. The idea was put forward by Friedman and Schwartz (1963), who found evidence for the mechanism in the build-up of US gold reserves. However, as Fremling (1985) pointed out, gold reserves rose simultaneously in the US and the rest of the world, implying that international linkages were working both ways. The evidence also suggests that the US balance of trade surpluses were falling rapidly during 1929–31. Simulation models of the transmission mechanisms of the world depression (Foreman-Peck *et al.*, 1992) suggest that the European economies would have avoided *only* 25 per cent of their historical losses during 1929–33 had the US maintained its 1929 level of production.

The importance of international institutions as a general-ised conditioning variable for generating the Great Depression has been emphasised in all the recent surveys of these events (Eichengreen, 1992; Temin, 1989). In particular, the working of the gold exchange standard in the late 1920s and its defence

---

9 Olney (1991) points out that one missed repayment was sufficient to result in the repossession of the durable good. Such a legal structure forced consumers to cut back new durable expenditure severely in the depression years 1929–33.
10 During this period the US was a relatively closed economy with low export and import ratios: during the 1920s the export–income ratio averaged 7 per cent of GDP and the import–income ratio 5 per cent of GDP.

during the critical period 1929–31 forced excessive deflation on the world economy. The gold exchange standard of the late 1920s failed to provide equilibrating adjustment mechanisms for surplus and deficit countries. The system generated asymmetric international adjustment; countries with surpluses on their balance of payments (such as the US and France) continued to accumulate surpluses while all the adjustment was forced on deficit countries. In order to defend the gold standard regime, real interest rates in the four major industrial countries (the US, Britain, France and Germany) rose from a mean of 3.7 per cent during 1924–9 to 10.5 per cent during 1930–2.

The realisation that the US depression cannot fully account for the world depression has resulted in explanations that consider the existence of *independent* depression forces from other regions and countries. The idea of an overproduction of primary commodities has received great attention in the inter-war literature. Kindleberger (1983) argued that an excess supply of primary commodities in the 1920s resulted in balance of payments constraints for primary producing economies, which acted to depress the demand for the goods of industrial countries. The empirical evidence for this hypothesis has been sought in the movement of the sectoral international **terms of trade** and in the build-up of primary commodity stocks during the 1920s.

An examination of the evidence raises some doubts about this mechanism. The sectoral terms of trade were not moving against primary producing economies during most of the 1920s (Solomou, 1987). Grilli and Yang's (1988) terms of trade data suggest that commodity prices collapsed only from 1928, as US overseas investment was redirected to the US stock market boom. This does not necessarily signal an overproduction of primary commodities during the 1920s. Similarly, although the stocks of primary commodities increased during 1925–9, this does not imply excess production. Rowe (1965) tried to measure excess stocks by considering the ratio of stocks to absorption (to capture demand effects on stock levels), and found that only three commodities showed a high ratio (sugar, wheat and coffee). Overproduction of primary commodities was not such a widespread problem to add an independent exogenous effect on the world depression. However, once depression started in 1928–9 the north–south linkages between the industrial and primary producing countries added important propagation mechanisms to the depression. The excess flexibility of primary commodity prices (relative to industrial goods prices) and the high level of initial indebtedness generated balance of payments and debt default problems in the 1930s that affected industrial countries.

Recent research on the forces generating depression in the other major industrial countries reinforces the idea that the US depression offers only a partial explanation for the world depression. Independent nation-specific depression forces were at work in a number of European countries, including Germany (Balderston, 1993; Borchart, 1991; James, 1986; Temin, 1971), France (Eichengreen, 1989) and Britain (Solomou and Weale, 1996).

Cyclical recovery, 1932–7
The recovery of the world economy during the 1930s can be dichotomised into two policy zones: the 'gold bloc' and the devaluing economies. While the average growth rates of these exchange rate blocs were similar during 1913–29 (and 1924–9), they saw marked differences in the 1930s. The devaluing countries were far more successful in their recoveries from the

Table 5 Exchange rates and GDP growth (percentage growth per annum)

	Gold bloc	Devaluers
1913–29	2.09	2.17
1929–37	0.32	1.68

Source: Solomou (1996, p. 116), using Maddison's (1982) GDP data.

world depression than the gold bloc economies (Table 5). Eichengreen (1991) considered evidence from a cross-section of countries: his classification distinguished four exchange rate zones, partly to reflect the new economic and trading blocs that developed in the 1930s and the different external constraints to economic growth. He distinguished the following groupings: the gold bloc, the exchange control countries, the sterling bloc and other depreciators. The results, reported in Table 6, show that during 1929–35 or 1929–36 the sterling bloc and the other devaluers grew much faster than the gold bloc and the exchange control countries. Such growth comparisons between the gold bloc and the devaluing countries suggest that the exchange rate regime had a major influence on economic recovery during the 1930s. Controlling for the amplitude of the depression, the average rate of economic growth of the non-gold-bloc countries was three percentage points greater than the performance of the gold bloc (Solomou, 1996).

The most direct effect of devaluation is expected to be on trade flows. Eichengreen and Sachs (1985) found a significant effect: countries which depreciated their currencies in the early 1930s succeeded in promoting recovery of export volumes compared with countries that remained committed to the gold standard over the period 1929–35.

Table 6 Change in industrial production, 1929–36 (in percentage points)

	1929–32	1929–33	1929–34	1929–35	1929–36
Gold bloc	-28.2	-22.6	-21.8	-20.6	-13.9
Exchange control	-35.7	-31.7	-21.2	-10.3	-2.3
Sterling bloc	-8.8	-2.5	8.9	18.1	27.8
Other depreciators	-17.5	-1.6	3.3	14.1	27.1

Source: Eichengreen (1991, p. 76).

Although a nominal devaluation gave an initial competitive advantage to the early devaluers, by 1937 much of this was eliminated by higher inflation rates in the early devaluing countries and by the devaluation of the gold bloc (Eichengreen and Sachs, 1985). Another relevant feature is that trade in the 1930s was increasingly being conducted in trading blocs with similar exchange rate strategies; hence, effective exchange rate changes were significantly dampened compared with bilateral and inter-bloc rates (Redmond, 1988). Thus, the performance of exports cannot help to explain why the devaluing countries performed relatively well during the complete business cycle upswing of 1932–7, and vice versa for the gold bloc. However, during the early recovery phase of 1932–5 there is a discernible *impact effect* on export performance: the early export recovery of the devaluing countries was better than that of the gold bloc economies.

The main link between devaluation and economic recovery in the 1930s is monetary policy. Before the devaluations of 1931, monetary policy in many European countries had been assigned to sustaining the fixed exchange rate regime. Once devaluation occurred, monetary policy was potentially freed as a policy instrument: the result was a major difference in the monetary policy of the countries leaving the gold standard relative to that of those remaining in the gold bloc. By 1933 a large differential had emerged in the monetary policy indicators of these two exchange rate zones: while the gold bloc witnessed monetary contraction, the devaluers saw expansion of money supply and falling interest rates. Eichengreen (1992) noted, however, the hesitation among the devaluers in pursuing expansionary monetary policies. The difference between the two exchange rate zones becomes significant only after a two-year lag, reflecting the association of depreciation with inflation (from the experience of the early 1920s) in the collective memory of the electorate and the political system.

Analysis

In the light of this descriptive overview of a number of cyclical phases during the inter-war period, I will now address the following analytical issues:

- Why were shocks during the period persistent in their effects?
- Why was volatility so much greater during the inter-war period relative to the previous 40 years?
- What is the balance between supply and demand shocks in causing business cycles?

Persistence of shocks
Many business cycle shocks during the inter-war period had persistent effects on aggregate macroeconomic performance. This feature is in marked contrast to the pre-1914 gold standard era, which saw the workings of a number of long-run adjustment processes resulting in the feature of macroeconomic

trend-stationarity. Examples of shocks that resulted in persistent effects are the 1920–1 depression in Britain, the German monetary stabilisation of 1923–4 and the Great Depression of 1929–33, which had long-term effects on a large number of economies.

Two key influences determined this new feature. First, the more discretionary policy framework of the inter-war period that arose out of the flexible exchange rate era (1919–25), combined with the attempts to re-establish the gold standard (in the form of the gold exchange standard), forced economies to deviate from their long-run paths on a permanent basis. This is very much at the heart of understanding the British and German experiences of the early 1920s. The maladjusted gold exchange standard has also been given a central role in explanations of the 1929–33 depression (Eichengreen, 1992; Temin, 1989). The defence of the fixed exchange rate regime by most countries during 1929–31 enforced excessive monetary and fiscal deflation. In the US this had a devastating effect on the stability of the financial system, with over one-third of all US banks failing between 1929 and 1933. The collapse of the financial system, combined with a high debt overhang from the 1920s, prevented a full revival of investment and consumer durable demand in the 1930s. Bernanke and James (1991) showed that this mechanism is a more general one. Countries that defended the gold standard for long periods raised the probability of financial crisis. Financial crisis is likely to have persistence effects by raising the cost of credit (Bernanke, 1983).

Secondly, the inter-war epoch did not have an equivalent set of international adjustment mechanisms to the pre-1914 era. It is important to stress that the pre-1914 gold standard survived for so long partly because there existed viable international adjustment mechanisms to nation-specific shocks, including international migration flows, trade protection and overseas investment (which stimulated the tradable sector). The inter-war era saw an abrupt end to many of these adjustment outlets. Legislative changes in the New World prevented mass emigration as a solution to mass unemployment; the disintegration of world trade, partly due to protection policies and a collapse of overseas investment during 1928–38, prevented export growth from stabilising the effect of domestic demand shocks. Instead of forcing adjustment (even if slow), severe business cycle shocks left economies permanently scarred with high unemployment and low output levels. Thus, the 'passing of the Kuznets cycle' (Abramovitz, 1968) in the inter-war era is of central importance to business cycle experiences, just as the presence of Kuznets swings before 1914 represented the workings of various stabilising cyclical adjustment mechanisms in the international economy.

Business cycle volatility

The evidence of high output volatility raises a number of questions: did the severity of shocks increase in the inter-war period relative to the past; was wage and price flexibility lower (forcing greater quantity adjustments on the economic system); did the transition to US economic leadership of the world economy transmit volatility to the rest of the world?

The nature of shocks did change significantly. Monetary policy shocks were of key importance: the flexible exchange rate era of 1919–25 was associated with a number of severe monetary and exchange rate variations; the malfunctioning gold exchange standard imposed excessive monetary deflation on the world economy between 1929 and 1933; the devalued exchange rates of the 1930s made possible the use of discretionary monetary policy to stimulate economic recovery.

The idea of maladjustments and inflexibilities in the labour market was emphasised by contemporaries. However, although wage rigidity was present in the inter-war era, it was also a feature of the pre-1914 era (Lewis, 1978). In an examination of the wage behaviour of Britain, France, Germany, the US and Sweden, Phelps Brown and Hopkins (1950) found that the degree of wage rigidity was comparable in the two periods in all these economies. More recent evidence suggests that only the US provides an example of increased wage rigidity in the inter-war period (an outcome of the New Deal labour market policies in the 1930s) relative to the pre-1914 era.

Increased volatility during the inter-war period was an international phenomenon. Kindleberger (1983) has attributed this to the leadership structure of the world economy after World War I. Although the US emerged from the war as the only major capital exporter, it was not willing to take the lead in stabilising the international economy. Kindleberger (1983) saw the contra-cyclical British overseas investment before 1914 as reflecting stabilising international behaviour. In contrast, the US followed a pro-cyclical pattern of overseas investment that destabilised the world economy. While Kindleberger viewed these features as a reflection of national leadership qualities, it seems more plausible that the existence of 'frontier' economies before 1914 made the absorption of capital by the world economy more likely. Given comparable profitability conditions, British investors would have responded in similar ways to their US counterparts during the inter-war period. The outcomes of the pre-1914 era were mainly fortuitous rather than planned; as in the inter-war period, these were the market outcomes of individuals seeking high rates of return.[11]

Supply-side and demand-side shocks
Both supply-side and demand-side shocks generated cyclical effects during this period. The survey of events in the 1920s and 1930s pointed to the impact of monetary policy and exchange rate shocks as demand-side shocks. As in the pre-1914 period, supply-side shocks arose from a variety of sources: labour market shocks played a key role in the early 1920s; during the 1930s supply shocks were propagated via financial markets in the form of financial crisis. The size of the agricultural sector in most of the major industrial countries was still large enough to transmit significant supply-side effects from weather shocks, as illustrated by the experience of the US during the 1920–1 depression (Romer, 1988). Quantitative research verifies these descriptive observations. Bayoumi and Eichengreen (1996) used a restricted VAR model to decompose supply and demand shocks for the US, Britain, Australia, Sweden and Denmark and found that demand and supply shocks were of comparable importance during the period 1919–38. Using monthly data for the US economy during 1913–40, Cecchetti and Karras (1994) found that while demand-side shocks were predominant before mid-1931, supply-side shocks (linked to the effects of banking collapse) played a more critical role after mid-1931.

11 One aspect of inter-war international capital flows that may have destabilised the world economy is the link between capital flows and the 'recycling' of reparation payments. Under the Dawes Plan of 1924 loans were granted to Germany to help finance reparation payments. The politicisation of international capital flows may have encouraged US investors to allocate more capital to Germany than was warranted by economic fundamentals.

Conclusions: inter-war period

- The key descriptive features of economic fluctuations during the inter-war period were quite different from those of the past. The amplitude, average period and persistence aspects of business cycles changed markedly: in the light of this, studies that attempt to model cyclical regularity over the long run are misleading.

- Inter-war fluctuations were influenced by both demand-side and supply-side shocks. Theoretical models to explain business cycles need to integrate both types of shock for a more complete understanding.

- Shocks generating business cycles also had *permanent* effects. Two major developments can account for these changes. First, the international adjustment mechanisms that were seen to operate in the classical gold standard era were no longer present. For example, restrictions to international migration imposed by the US and other countries of the New World prevented adjustment in the labour market. Secondly, protectionism prevented export revival from playing a central role during the depressed conditions of the 1930s. The passing of the long-swing international adjustment mechanisms had a significant effect on the nature of the inter-war cyclical process relative to that observed before 1914.

- The policy regimes of the inter-war period had a significant effect on conditioning the nature of cyclical fluctuations. The flexible exchange rate period of 1919–25, the defence of the gold standard during 1928–33 and the currency devaluations of the 1930s help us to understand the nature of cyclical events during this period.

- The world depression is best understood as the outcome of a cluster of independent causal processes. The most convincing international mechanism relates to the defence of the maladjusted gold exchange standard. Beyond this common factor, a cluster of adverse nation-specific shocks in the US and Europe helps to explain the uniqueness of this event in economic history.

• Given the severity of the world depression of 1929–33 and the structural changes in the cyclical adjustment mechanisms, a new role can be seen for economic policy as a means for activating economic recovery. The comparative performance of the gold bloc and more activist policy regimes suggests that the latter were more effective in inducing economic recovery during the 1930s.

Post-war business cycles

Post-war stylised facts

Business cycle amplitudes
Table 2 (p. 32) shows that there has been a marked reduction in the variance of macroeconomic output fluctuations in the post-war era relative to the inter-war era. The volatility of the post-war period is also lower than for the pre-1914 era, suggesting that post-war policies and long-run structural changes (such as the growth in the size of the government sector) may have generated stabilising effects on modern economies (Burns, 1960; Tobin, 1980; Zarnowitz, 1992).

Some recent work has, however, questioned the comparability of these long-run data series. For example, Romer (1986) has argued that the high variance of the pre-1914 US economy is largely a statistical artefact, resulting from Simon Kuznets's estimation methods for US gross national product (GNP). Romer has revised the existing macroeconomic series on the assumption that they have an artificially high variance for the pre-1914 period. Simon Kuznets (1946) estimated an annual series of GNP using regression analysis. The regression series was constructed by taking the period 1909–38, for which fairly reliable estimates of GNP can be obtained using the income–expenditure approach. Kuznets regressed the percentage deviation from trend of GNP on the percentage deviation from trend for aggregate commodity production.[12] He then used the estimated coefficient to form an estimate of GNP for the period 1869–1918. However, the regression for the period 1909–38 is heavily influenced by the depression of the 1930s. Thus the constructed series may be biased to generating large cyclical variations. The percentage deviations from trend of GNP and commodity output move much closer to 1:1 during the 1930s than for other periods. During 1909–28 the coefficient is only 0.6. Romer (1986) used the coefficient for the period 1909–28 as the basis for constructing the GNP series and this yields a substantially less volatile series before 1929. In the light of the revised data, Romer argued that the depression of the 1930s was exceptional and nothing comparable can be found before 1929. In fact, the variance of US business cycles for the period 1870–1929 looks comparable to that for the post-war era, questioning the idea that demand management has moderated cyclical fluctuations since World War II.

There are, however, a number of problems with Romer's data revisions. If we assume that the macroeconomic relationships of the period 1870–1909 are similar to those for the period 1909–28, then we observe a significantly lower amplitude than in the original Kuznets series. However, it is unlikely

---

12 Commodity production is a composite index of industrial and agricultural production.

that these quantitative relationships will remain stable over such long periods. Moreover, the existence of long swings in the US economy suggests that Romer's revisions are unlikely to be correct because the period 1909–28 is mainly capturing an upswing in the US economy; the 1930s may be more relevant to depicting depression phases, such as 1890s. Romer's assumptions are likely to have introduced artificial stability in the output data for the period before World War I.

Accepting the need to revise the US national income data, Balke and Gordon (1989) have constructed a GNP series using new information on distribution, construction and consumer prices. Their results suggest that the variance of the pre-1914 economy is 1.77 times greater than for the post-war period. Although this is lower than that from the original Kuznets data, the results suggest that the pre-1914 economy was far more volatile than that in the post-war era, reinforcing the conventional picture.

Table 2 also shows that the phenomenon of a low variance during the post-war period is observed in a large number of countries, with very different historical data construction methods. It would be difficult to argue that all these long-run changes are a statistical artefact (Backus and Kehoe, 1992; Sheffrin, 1988). Thus, although measurement errors make it difficult to compare long-run historical data, the evidence is consistent with the idea of a structural shift towards relatively low business cycle volatility after World War II.

Cyclical durations
Cyclical durations averaged three- to five-year growth cycles during the golden age of the 1950s and 1960s (Zarnowitz, 1992). Although short **inventory cycles** have been observed for the pre-war period, such a short duration for the major

economic cycle is historically unique. The average length of the cycle has increased significantly since the 1970s. Analysing data for 1960–86 using the statistical method of the maximum entropy spectrum to determine cyclical durations for the economies of countries belonging to the Organization for Economic Cooperation and Development (OECD), Hillinger (1992) found that cycles have increased in duration, although average durations vary significantly across countries. A large number of countries were influenced by a medium-term cycle of 12–15 years.[13] The evidence suggests that cyclical durations have not been stable even within the post-war era, with a discernible shift in average durations since the late 1960s. Although most business cycle theories do not seek to explain a regular periodic cycle, the observation of shifting mean cyclical durations suggests that the adjustment processes to shocks and/or the nature of shocks change over time.

International synchronisation

The post-war business cycle was not a world economic cycle; instead, bilateral cyclical linkages can be seen across a variety of countries. Table 4 (p. 34) shows very strong bilateral co-movements between Britain and the US, Japan and the US, Canada and the US, Germany and Britain, and Canada and Britain. Insignificant linkages are observed between Japan and Britain, Japan and Germany, and Japan and Canada. Such strong bilateral cyclical linkages are in marked contrast to the inter-war era, when the business cycle is far more of an international phenomenon (Backus and Kehoe, 1992).

---

13 Most countries were also influenced by a short cycle of five to ten years and a shorter inventory cycle. As noted above, a multiplicity of cycles was also the norm in the gold standard period.

Using less formal statistical methods, Zarnowitz (1981) compared the business cycle timings of the US, Canada, Britain, Germany and Japan within the National Bureau **reference cycle** framework for 1948–80. He also found strong co-movements between different sets of countries, such as the US and Canada, and Britain and Germany, rather than an international business cycle affecting all the major countries simultaneously.

Using quarterly output data for a larger cross-section of countries for the period 1959–89, Danthine and Donaldson (1993) documented both bilateral and international business cycle linkages. At the bilateral level there were some very strong cyclical co-variations. For example, Germany showed significant co-movements with Austria, France, Italy, Switzerland and Britain; Britain had strong bilateral linkages with France and Germany. Aggregating the countries of the European Community (EC) into one bloc we can also compare how each individual EC member varies with the EC bloc. The co-movements are very much weaker, suggesting that it is strong bilateral ties that are important in the intra-European cyclical linkages, not bloc behaviour. Comparing the individual EC members with the US, their linkages have been far stronger than with the EC bloc. The data also allow us to compare inter-bloc cyclical influences: comparing the cyclical variations of the EC, the US and Japan, we see strong positive co-movements across these three major economic zones. At this level of aggregation there is some evidence of international business cycle linkages.

Price–output cyclical co-movements
In the light of developments in the monetary theory of business cycles (Lucas, 1977) and the real business cycle theory (Kydland

and Prescott, 1982), the cyclical relationship between prices and output is central to business cycle research. Lucas simply *assumed* that prices move pro-cyclically with output as a stylised fact. Analysis of the post-war data suggests the very opposite, with price and output fluctuations moving contra-cyclically (Danthine and Donaldson, 1993).

However, evidence from other historical eras does not suggest stability of this relationship in the long run. During the classical gold standard period, price–output fluctuations did not show any consistent positive or negative pattern; the inter-war period was chiefly characterised by pro-cyclical movements; the post-war phase up to the 1970s was dominated by contra-cyclical movements. The most recent period suggests further changes. Pro-cyclical movements have been observed in the US and the European economies in the 1980s and 1990s; as an example, the depression of the early 1990s in the major industrial economies resulted in the lowest inflation rates since the 1960s.

Pro-cyclicality, contra-cyclicality and non-cyclicality are all possible stylised facts, depending on the historical period being observed. The aims of theoretical frameworks should be to determine the reasons for the observed shifts in this relation-ship across different historical periods. Theoretical discussions that have sought to explain a universal stylised fact are, thus, misleading.

The evidence raises a number of theoretical and empirical questions that need to be considered further. For example, pro-cyclical price–output fluctuations arise in the inter-war period and in some phases of the post-1973 epoch; both phases are periods of monetary policy discretion and unsettled exchange rates. In contrast, during the classical gold standard period and the Bretton Woods era the leading economies sustained fixed exchange rates, limiting national policy discretion. Thus, a *prima facie* case can be established that the structural shifts in price–output movements are, at least partly, determined by the monetary/exchange rate policy regime. This does not mean that the price–output relationship is not subject to real business cycle influences, such as the effects of technology and other supply-side shocks. What it does mean is that in some periods these effects are of secondary importance to the policy regime.

Disaggregated business cycle volatilities
Zarnowitz (1985, p. 525) defines business cycles as 'expansions and contractions that consist of patterns of recurrent, serially correlated and cross correlated movements in many economic (and even other) activities'. This captures the general features of co-movement in a number of important economic variables. For example, investment, consumption and aggregate output co-move over the business cycle. This, in itself, may seem a rather intuitive and uninteresting result. However, a further stylised fact has a central role in business cycle discussions: it is often argued that there is a regular variance structure to the disaggregated data, with investment volatility being greater than aggregate volatility. The phenomenon of *consumption smoothing* by individuals, as predicted by the permanent income and life cycle hypotheses, implies that consumption is expected to be the least volatile component of aggregate demand.

Empirical studies generally accept this description of the structure of the disaggregated data (Hillinger, 1992; Kydland and Prescott, 1982; Lucas, 1977). However, a number of important 'outliers' to this generalisation need to be noted. The US Great Depression of the 1930s cannot be understood without an explanation of consumption volatility far in excess of investment fluctuations (Calomiris, 1993; Temin, 1976,

1989). Similarly, to account for the boom and depression of the 1980s and 1990s in both the US and Europe we need to be able to explain the observed consumption shifts (Blanchard, 1993; Hall, 1993). These two events in history carry much weight in terms of their impact on the economics and politics of market economies. The depression of the 1930s is historically unique in terms of its severity and the depression of the early 1990s is the most severe downturn for 50 years. To focus exclusively on investment volatility as an explanation of business cycle fluctuations is incomplete in that there is a selection bias towards neglecting information from major depressions. Thus, although consumption smoothing is an important empirical feature that needs to be integrated into business cycle research, *episodic* consumption volatility also needs to be integrated into a broader picture. Explaining these consumption shifts, or at the very least recognising their economic implications, is essential if we are to understand some of the major business cycle fluctuations of the twentieth century. Moreover, the financial deregulation which has been taking place since the 1980s means that consumption behaviour is likely to play an increasingly important role in business cycle fluctuations in the future.

This empirical survey has focused on a few of the stylised facts that will prove to be central to our evaluation of explanations for post-war business cycles. It is to these explanatory frameworks that we now turn.

Explanations of post-war business cycles

Monetary frameworks
The modern version of the monetary theory of business cycles was developed in the 1970s and early 1980s (Barro, 1981;

Lucas, 1977), although strands of these ideas can be found in earlier work (Hayek, 1933). The explanation is embedded in the New Classical rational expectations framework. Within this approach an *anticipated* monetary event has no effect on the economic behaviour of individuals. However, a random (unanticipated) monetary shock induces agents to change their decisions to work, consume and invest. Although expectations are determined by the rational expectations rule, individuals do not acquire all information instantaneously, since gathering information has a cost (if only an opportunity cost). Absolute price changes, resulting from monetary policy shocks, are likely to be mistaken for relative price changes that will have real effects. Hence, inflationary monetary shocks will have an expansionary real effect over the business cycle; this effect will be temporary because, with time, individuals realise that they have mistaken an absolute price change for a relative one. Consider Lucas's model as an example of how monetary shocks are propagated to generate economic cycles. The model is presented in Box 1.

Equation 1 in Box 1 implies that the economy has a tendency, once shocked, to return to a steady trend path: cycles are modelled as transitory deviations about the trend. Although deviations may arise between the actual price level and the rational expectation prediction of the price level, the rational expectations framework implies that the deviations will follow a random process about the trend. Lucas models the effect of an unanticipated monetary shock using the 'island market' parable; the general idea behind this concept is that individuals have more information about their particular activities of production than about other activities. The parable is a way of rationalising the idea that individuals have incomplete information, which results in a signal extraction

Box 1   A monetary model

The Lucas supply function implies:

$$Y_t = Y_{nt} + \alpha(P_t - P^*_t) + \varepsilon_t \tag{1}$$

where:

Y_t = income;
Y_{nt} = steady-state income;
P_t = price level;
P^*_t = rational expectations prediction of price level;
ε_t = random error.

The trend specification is:

$$Y_{nt} = \beta + \gamma_{\text{trend}} \tag{2}$$

The cyclical variations are given by:

$$Y_{ct} = \alpha(P_t - P^*_t) + \varepsilon_t \tag{3}$$

problem, with producers mistaking absolute price changes for relative price changes, distorting real behaviour. The signal extraction problem sets off a cyclical propagation mechanism as individuals respond to inflationary shocks by raising investment and labour supply. However, once more information is processed individuals will realise that their investment and labour supply decisions are non-optimal, resulting in a downward cyclical correction.

Although the model can produce an explanation of some of the basic features of business cycles, including autocorrelation in economic data and co-movement of variables, a number of serious empirical problems remain. Let us evaluate these problems in the light of the post-war stylised facts we have set out above.

Gordon (1986) rejects the relevance of Lucas's approach on both theoretical and empirical grounds. At the theoretical level it is difficult to accept the continuous market-clearing assumption of the framework in the light of the existence of involuntary unemployment over the business cycle.[14] At the empirical level the theory is clearly unable to explain the cyclical durations we have observed in the post-war period, and faces even greater difficulties in explaining events such as the depression of the 1930s. Governments provide the public with monthly money supply figures. Within Lucas's framework, the frequency of this information could yield an explanation for a high-frequency cycle (within a year), but it would be difficult to account for business cycle durations of five or ten years that have characterised the post-war era.

The clearest inconsistency between the theory and the evidence relates to the price–output cyclical relationship. The Lucas monetary misperception model relies on a positive cyclical co-movement of prices and output. For most of the post-war period the relationship has been a contra-cyclical one. The evidence of pro-cyclical price–output movements in the 1980s and 1990s suggests that monetary factors may be more important in this era. However, the transmission mechanism of monetary policy in this period needs to incorporate a more extended framework than that offered by Lucas if we are to

14 Another theoretical critique is that Lucas's model is incomplete in its treatment of demand and supply responses. For example, although the belief that a current price or wage is high may increase supply of labour and goods, a symmetric model would imply that consumer demand and labour demand should fall, leaving aggregate output and employment little changed.

account for *major* depressions. In particular, the role of debt accumulation and debt overhang in generating consumption volatility in the business cycles of the 1980s and 1990s is of central importance.

Time-series analysis of macroeconomic data also raises doubts about the basic structure of Lucas's model. Lucas works with a model that has a unique supply-side equilibrium growth path. Nelson and Plosser (1982) found that most US macroeconomic data could be described as random walks. Their test involved using the parametric Dickey–Fuller test for trend-stationarity. Perron and Phillips (1987) developed a non-parametric procedure for testing for random walks; they reject the random walk idea for data from before World War II but fail to reject it for the post-war period. Similar tests for trend-stationarity in other countries reinforce the US findings (Mills and Taylor, 1989; Mullineux *et al.*, 1993; Walton, 1988). Clearly, the evidence of random walks means that shocks have permanent or highly persistent effects. Lucas's model, which describes cycles as transitory processes, is inconsistent with this result. It should be noted, however, that this result cannot be logically interpreted as a general rejection of monetary explanations. What this suggests is that the analysis of monetary propagation needs to provide an explanation of possible persistence channels of monetary policy.

Real business cycle perspectives
In the light of the failings of monetary explanations of business cycles, the 1980s saw the development of real business cycle (RBC) theory as a way of accounting for the observed stylised facts. Instead of focusing on monetary shocks, the RBC literature drew attention to the cyclical impact of technological and other supply-side shocks. The theory has three main

features: first, in the light of the evidence of **non-trend-stationary** economic data, the analysis of economic growth and business cycles is integrated into a single framework; secondly, within a propagation–impulse framework, the theory emphasises the importance of impulses (shocks) rather than endogenous cyclical processes; finally, the theory offers an equilibrium perspective to business cycles.

To illustrate the basic strands of RBC theory, consider the effects of a *random* technological shock that has a favourable effect on the economy. Since technological improvement raises productivity and output, such a shock allows the representative individual to increase current consumption. However, the individual also values extra consumption in the future; in order to smooth consumption over time the individual will increase investment as a way of also raising future consumption. Hence, even a purely random technological shock will generate cyclical adjustments via the inter-temporal nature of decision making acting as a cyclical propagation mechanism.

Extending this basic model, consider a more realistic second approximation, allowing for the effects of *persistent* technology shocks in a simple growth process:

$$Y_t = \alpha + \beta\, Y_{t-1} + U_t \tag{1}$$

$$U_t = g + U_{t-1} + \varepsilon_t \tag{2}$$

where Y_t is aggregate output, U_t is the path of technology and ε_t is a random error. Equations (1) and (2) describe a random walk in output by specifying that the technological path grows at a rate g with a random walk in the level of technology. This yields a growth process that generates a random walk in output. By integrating the analysis of economic growth and business cycles the RBC framework is able to account for the observed random walk in aggregate output.

It is recognised that very large supply-side shocks are required if such explanations are going to account for the observed business cycle fluctuations. For example, consider a favourable supply-side shock that raises GDP by 1 per cent. If half of this is saved and the rate of return is as high as 10 per cent, the impact on GDP in the next period is reduced to only 0.05 per cent (Blanchard and Fischer, 1989). Even a large *random* technological shock has limited propagation effects.

Can such technology shocks explain post-war business cycles? Most of the recent literature has used the Solow TFP residual to measure the variance of technology shocks. Although, in general, the Solow residual reproduces the cyclical path of economies it is extremely difficult to distinguish supply-side shocks from demand-side shocks. Productivity shifts can be accounted for by so-called 'off the production function behaviour' (Mankiw, 1989); for example, if firms hoard labour and capital during recessions, TFP will rise in a boom and fall in recessions without technological shocks being observed.

Perhaps the most serious problem with RBC explanations of business cycles is the assumption that involuntary unemployment is ruled out by the theory. For the theory to explain the large unemployment swings requires a very large elasticity of labour supply with respect to real wages, which contradicts microeconomic estimates. Overall, the theory seems unable to explain a number of business cycle features.

Conclusions: post-war period

• Although there is a tendency among economists to speak of business cycle regularities, the evidence considered suggests that many of the defining features of post-war business cycles are time specific. Durations, amplitudes and causal processes have changed significantly relative to previous periods. There is also evidence to show that these features have changed significantly since 1973 relative to the post-war 'golden age' (1950–73). Such changes are the norm, invalidating the usefulness of stylised facts as anything more than a description of historically specific details.

- Monetary shocks were more important in the post-1973 era than in the Bretton Woods era. To dismiss the role of money in business cycle fluctuations based on studies of the early post-war period is highly misleading as a general policy guide. Considering all the historical evidence shows us that the impact of monetary policy shocks has shifted over time and across different policy regimes.

- Existing theories of cyclical fluctuations have provided an incomplete understanding of post-war cycles. This failure is partly an outcome of the restrictive assumptions and a failure to recognise that one type of shock is unlikely to explain cyclical fluctuations. Structural and policy regime changes have acted as important filters to the impact of particular types of shock.

Appendix. The Kalman filter

Structural time-series models (such as the Kalman filter) are explicitly set up in terms of analysing unobserved trend and cyclical components (Harvey, 1985, 1989; Harvey and Jaeger, 1993). Following this approach, a time-series can be modelled as:

$$y_t = \mu_t + \psi_t + \varepsilon_t$$

where:

$$\mu_t = \mu_{t-1} + \beta_{t-1} + \xi_{t-1}$$
$$\beta_t = \beta_{t-1} + \nu_t$$
$$\psi_t = (1 - \rho\cos\lambda L)\omega_t + (\rho\sin\lambda L)\omega_t^* / (1 - 2\rho\cos\lambda L + \rho^2 L^2)$$

μ_t stands for the trend component of y_t; ξ_t allows the trend to shift up and down; ν_t accounts for shocks to the slope, β_t; ψ_t captures the cyclical regularities in y_t; L represents the lag operator; ω_t represents the shocks to the cyclical component; ε_t accounts for short-term erratic movements and possible measurement errors in y_t. ε_t, ξ_t, ν_t and ω_t are assumed to be mutually independent white noise processes, with ω_t^* arising by construction under the constraint that $\sigma(\omega) = \sigma(\omega^*)$; λ is the frequency of the cycle and ρ is the damping factor. Koopman *et al.* (1995) outline the procedures for implementing the Kalman filter allowing us to estimate up to three cycles in the data.

Bibliography

Abramovitz, M. (1968) 'The Passing of the Kuznets Cycle', *Economica*, 35, 349–67.

Adelman, I. (1960) 'Business Cycles – Endogenous or Stochastic', *Economic Journal*, 70, 783–96.

Aldcroft, D. H. and Fearon, P. (Eds) (1972) *British Economic Fluctuations, 1790–1939*, London.

Backus, D. K. and Kehoe, P. J. (1992) 'International Evidence on the Historical Properties of Business Cycles', *American Economic Review*, 82, 864–88.

Balassa, B. (1964) 'The Purchasing Power Parity Doctrine: A Reappraisal', *Journal of Political Economy*, 72, 584–96.

Balderston, T. (1993) *The Origins and Course of the German Economic Crisis, 1923–32*, Berlin.

Balke, N. S. and Gordon, R. J. (1989) 'The Estimation of Prewar Gross National Product: Methodology and New Evidence', *Journal of Political Economy*, 97, 38–92.

68 Economic cycles

4

Barro, R. J. (1981) *Money, Expectations, and Business Cycles*, New York.

Barro, R. J. (1989) *Modern Business Cycle Theory*, Cambridge, Mass.

Barro, R. J. and Hercowitz, Z. (1980) 'Money Stock Revisions and Unanticipated Monetary Growth', *Journal of Monetary Economics*, 6, 257–67.

Bayoumi, T. and Eichengreen, B. (1996) 'The Gold Standard and the International Monetary System', in T. Bayoumi, B. Eichengreen and M. P. Taylor (Eds), *Modern Perspectives on the Gold Standard*, Cambridge.

Bernanke, B. S. (1983) 'Nonmonetary Effects of the Financial Crisis in the Propagation of the Great Depression', *American Economic Review*, 73, 257–76.

Bernanke, B. S. (1986) 'Alternative Explanations of the Money–Income Correlation', *Carnegie-Rochester Conference Series on Public Policy*, 25, 49–100.

Bernanke, B. S. and James, H. (1991) 'The Gold Standard, Deflation and Financial Crisis in the Great Depression: An International Comparison', in R. G. Hubbard (Ed.), *Financial Crisis*, Chicago.

Blackburn, K. and Ravn, M. O. (1992) 'Business Cycles in the UK: Facts and Fictions', *Economica*, 59, 383–401.

Blanchard, O. (1993) 'Consumption and the Recession of 1990–1991', *American Economic Review*, 83, 270–4.

Blanchard, O. J. and Fischer, S. (1989) *Lectures in Macroeconomics*, Cambridge, Mass.

Blanchard, O. J. and Watson, M. W. (1986) 'Are Business Cycles All Alike?', in R. J. Gordon (Ed.), *The American Business Cycle*, Chicago.

Borchart, K. (1991) *Perspectives on Modern German Economic History and Policy*, Cambridge.

Broadberry, S. N. (1984) 'The North European Depression in the 1920s', *Scandinavian Economic History Review*, 32, 159–67.

Broadberry, S. N. (1986) *The British Economy Between the Wars: A Macroeconomic Survey*, Oxford.

Burns, A. F. (1960) 'Progress Towards Economic Stability', *American Economic Review*, 50, 1–19.

Cairncross, A. K. (1953) *Home and Foreign Investment, 1870–1913: Studies in Capital Accumulation*, Cambridge.

Calomiris, C. W. (1993) 'Financial Factors in the Great Depression', *Journal of Economic Perspectives*, 7, 2.

Campbell, J. Y. and Mankiw, N. W. (1987) 'Are Output Fluctuations Transitory?', *Quarterly Journal of Economics*, 102, 857–80.

Capie, F. (1990) 'Money and Business Cycles in Britain 1870–1913', in N. Velupellai and N. Thygesen (Eds), *Business Cycles, Non Linearities, Disequilibrium, and Simulations: Readings in Business Cycles Theory*, London.

Capie, F. and Mills, T. C. (1991) 'Money and Business Cycles in the U.S. and U.K., 1870 to 1913', *Manchester School*, 53 (supplement), 38–56.

Capie, F. and Mills, T. C. (1992) 'Money and Business Cycles in the United States, 1870 to 1913: A Reexamination of Friedman and Schwartz', *Explorations in Economic History*, 29, 251–73.

Catao, L. A. V. and Solomou, S. N. (1993) 'Business Cycles During the Gold Standard, 1870–1913', Department of Applied Economics Working Paper, No. 9304, Cambridge University.

Cecchetti, S. G. and Karras, G. (1994) 'Sources of Output Fluctuations During the Interwar Period: Further Evidence on the Causes of the Great Depression', *Review of Economics and Statistics*, 77, 80–102.

Clarke, H. (1847) 'Physical Economy – A Preliminary Inquiry into the Physical Laws Governing the Periods of Famine and Panics', *Railway Register*.

Cogley, T. and Nason, J. M. (1995) 'Effects of the Hodrick and Prescott Filter on Trend and Difference Stationary Time Series: Implications for Business Cycle Research', *Journal of Economic Dynamics and Control*, 19, 253–78.

Cooley, T. F. and Ohanian, L. E. (1991) 'The Cyclical Behaviour of Prices', *Journal of Monetary Economics*, 28, 25–60.

Crafts, N. F. R., Leybourne, S. J. and Mills, T. C. (1989) 'The Climacteric in Late Victorian Britain and France: A Reappraisal of Evidence', *Journal of Applied Econometrics*, 4, 103–18.

Crafts, N. F. R. and Mills, T. C. (1992) 'Economic Fluctuations, 1851–1913: A Perspective Based on Growth Theory', in S. N. Broadberry and N. F. R. Crafts (Eds), *Britain in the World Economy 1870–1939*, Cambridge.

Danthine, J. P. and Donaldson, J. B. (1993) 'Methodological and Empirical Issues in Real Business Cycle Theory', *European Economic Review*, 37, 1–36.

Dowie, J. (1975) '1919–20 is in Need of Attention', *Economic History Review*, 28, 429–50.

Eichenbaum, M. and Singleton, K. J. (1986) 'Do Equilibrium Real Business Cycle Theories Explain Postwar US Business Cycles?', *NBER Macroeconomics Annual*, Cambridge, Mass.

Eichengreen, B. J. (1983) 'The Causes of British Business Cycles, 1833–1913', *Journal of European Economic History*, 12, 145–61.

Eichengreen, B. J. (1986) 'Understanding 1921–27: Inflation and Economic Recovery in the 1920s', *Rivista Di Storia Economica, New Series*, 5, 34–66.

Eichengreen, B. J. (1989) 'The Political Economy of the Smoot Hawley Tariff', *Research in Economic History*, 11, 1–44.

Eichengreen, B. J. (1991) 'Relaxing the External Constraint: Europe in the 1930s', in G. Alogoskoufis, L. Papademos and R. Portes (Eds), *External Constraints on Macroeconomic Policy: The European Experience*, Cambridge.

Eichengreen, B. J. (1992) *Golden Fetters: The Gold Standard and the Great Depression, 1919–1939*, Oxford.

Eichengreen, B. J. (1994) 'History of the International Monetary System: Implications for Research in International Macroeconomics and Finance', in F. Van Der Ploeg, *The Handbook of International Macroeconomics*, Oxford.

Eichengreen, B. J. and Sachs, J. (1985) 'Exchange Rates and Economic Recovery in the 1930s', *Journal of Economic History*, 45, 925–46.

Feinstein, C. H., Matthews, R. C. O. and Odling-Smee, J. (1982) 'The Timing of the Climacteric and its Sectoral Incidence in the UK 1873–1913', in C. P. Kindleberger and C. Di Tella (Eds), *Economics in the Long View: Essays in Honour of W. W. Rostow*, Vol. 3, London.

Fleisig, H. (1972) 'The U.S. and the Non-European Periphery during the Early Years of the Great Depression', in H. Van Der Wee (Ed.), *The Great Depression Revisited*, The Hague.

Ford, A. G. (1981) 'Trade Cycles, 1870–1914', in R. Floud and D. N. McCloskey (Eds), *The Economic History of Britain Since 1700*, Vol. 2, Cambridge.

Foreman-Peck, J., Hughes-Hallett, A. and Ma, Y. (1992) 'The Transmission of the Great Depression in the United States, Britain, France and Germany', *European Economic Review*, 36, 685–94.

Fremling, G. M. (1985) 'Did the U.S. Transmit the Great Depression to the Rest of the World?', *American Economic Review*, 75, 1181–5.

Friedman, M. and Schwartz, A. J. (1963) *A Monetary History of the United States 1867–1960*, Princeton.

Friedman, M. and Schwartz, A. J. (1982) *Monetary Trends in the United States and the United Kingdom*, Chicago.

Frisch, R. (1933) 'Propagation and Impulse Problems in Dynamic Economics', in R. Frisch (Ed.), *Essays in Honour of Gustav Cassel*, London.

Gordon, R. J. (ed.) (1986) *The American Business Cycle: Continuity and Change*, Chicago.

Greenwald, B. C. and Stiglitz, J. E. (1988) 'Examining Alternative Economic Theories', *Brooking Papers on Economic Activity*, 1, 207–60.

Grilli, E. R. and Yang, M. C. (1988) 'Primary Commodity Prices, Manufactured Goods Prices and the Terms of Trade of Developing Countries', *World Bank Economic Review*, 1, 1–47.

Hall, R. E. (1993) 'Macro Theory and the Recession of 1990–1991', *American Economic Review*, 83, 275–9.

Harvey, A. C. (1985) 'Trends and Cycles in Macroeconomic Time Series', *Journal of Business and Economic Statistics*, 3, 216–27.

Harvey, A. C. (1989) *Forecasting, Structural Time Series Models and the Kalman Filter*, Cambridge.

Harvey, A. C. and Jaeger, A. (1993) 'Detrending, Stylized Facts and the Business Cycle', *Journal of Applied Econometrics*, 8, 231–47.

Hatton, T. (1990) 'The Demand For British Exports, 1870–1913', *Economic History Review*, 43, 576–96.

Hayek, P. A. (1933) *Monetary Theory and the Trade Cycle*, London.

Hicks, J. R. (1974) 'Real and Monetary Factors in Economic Fluctuations', *Scottish Journal of Political Economy*, 21, 205–14.

Hicks, J. R. (1982) 'Are There Economic Cycles?', in J. R. Hicks, *Money, Interest and Wages: Collected Essays on Economic Theory*, Vol. 2, Oxford.

Hillinger, C. (ed.) (1992) *Cyclical Growth in Market and Planned Economies*, Oxford.

Holtfrerich, C-L. (1986) 'US Capital Exports to Germany, 1919–1923 Compared to 1924–1929', *Explorations in Economic History*, 23, 1–32.

James, H. (1986) *The German Slump: Politics and Economics 1924–1936*, Oxford.

Jevons, W. S. (1884) *Investigations in Currency and Finance*, London.

Jones, E. L. (1964) *Seasons and Prices*, London.

Khatri, Y. and Solomou, S. N. (1996) 'Climate and Fluctuations in Agricultural Output, 1867–1913', Department of Applied Economics Working Paper, No. 9617, Cambridge University.

Kindleberger, C. P. (1983) *The World in Depression, 1929–1939*, London.

King, R. G. and Plosser, C. I. (1984) 'Money Credit and Prices in a Real Business Cycle Economy', *American Economic Review*, 74, 363–80.

Koopman, S. J., Harvey, A. C., Doornik, J. A. and Shephard, N. (1995)

Stamp 5.0: Structural Time Series Analyser, Modeller and Predictor, London.

Kuznets, S. S. (1946) *National Product Since 1869,* New York.

Kydland, F. E. and Prescott, E. C. (1982) 'Time to Build and Aggregate Fluctuations', *Econometrica,* 50, 1345–70.

Lewis, W. A. (1978) *Growth and Fluctuations 1870–1913,* London.

Long, J. B. and Plosser, C. I. (1983) 'Real Business Cycles', *Journal of Political Economy,* 91, 39–69.

Lucas, R. E. (1975) 'An Equilibrium Model of the Business Cycle', *Journal of Political Economy,* 83, 1113–44.

Lucas, R. E. (1977) 'Understanding Business Cycles', in K. Brunner and A. H. Meltzer (Eds), *Stabilisation of the Domestic and International Economy,* Carnegie-Rochester Conference Series on Public Policy 5, Amsterdam.

Lucas, R. E. (1981) *Studies in Business Cycle Theory,* Cambridge, Mass.

Lucas, R. E. (1987) *Models of Business Cycles.* Yrjo Jahnsson Lectures, Oxford.

Maddison, A. (1982) *Phases of Capitalist Development,* Oxford.

Maddison, A. (1991) *Dynamic Forces in Capitalist Development,* Oxford.

Mankiw, N. G. (1989) 'Real Business Cycles', *Journal of Economic Perspectives,* 3, 79–90.

Matthews, R. C. O. (1959) *The Business Cycle,* Cambridge.

Matthews, R. C. O., Feinstein, C. and Odling-Smee, J. (1982) *British Economic Growth,* Oxford.

Maunder, W. J. (1986) *The Uncertainty Business: Risks and Opportunities in Weather and Climate,* London.

McCallum, B. T. (1986) 'On Real and Sticky-Price Theories of the Business Cycle', *Journal of Money, Credit and Banking,* 18, 397–414.

Mills, T. (1991) 'Are Fluctuations in UK Output Transitory or Permanent?', *Manchester School,* 59, 1–11.

Mills, T. and Taylor, M. P. (1989) 'Random Walk Components in Output and Exchange Rates: Some Robust Tests on UK Data', *Bulletin of Economic Research,* 41, 215–42.

Mullineux, A. W. and Dickinson, D. G. (1992) 'Real Business Cycles: Theory and Evidence', *Journal of Economic Surveys,* 6, 321–58.

Mullineux, A. W., Dickinson, D. and Peng, W. (1993) *Business Cycles,* Oxford.

Nelson, C. R. and Plosser, C. I. (1982) 'Trends and Random Walks in Macro-Economic Time Series', *Journal of Monetary Economics,* 10, 139–62.

Olney, M. L. (1991) *Buy Now Pay Later: Advertising, Credit and Consumer Durables in the 1920s*, London.

Patat, J. P. and Luttala, M. (1990) *A Monetary History of France in the Twentieth Century*, London.

Perron, P. (1989) 'The Great Crash, the Oil Price Shock and the Unit Root Hypothesis', *Econometrica*, 56, 1361–401.

Perron, P. and Phillips, P. C. B. (1987) 'Does GNP Have a Unit Root?', *Economics Letters*, 23, 139–45.

Phelps Brown, E. H. and Hopkins, S. V. (1950) 'The Course of Wage-Rates in Five Countries, 1860–1939', *Oxford Economic Papers*, 2, 226–96.

Plosser, C. (1989) 'Understanding Real Business Cycles', *Journal of Economic Perspectives*, 3, 3.

Pollard, S. (1989) *Britain's Prime and Britain's Decline: The British Economy 1870–1914*, London.

Prior, M. J. (1989) 'Weather Interference with Construction Operations: Met Office Climatological Services', in S. J. Harrison and K. Smith (Eds), *Weather Sensitivity and Services in Scotland*, Edinburgh.

Redmond, J. (1988) 'Effective Exchange Rates in the Nineteen-Thirties: North America and the Gold Bloc', *Journal of European Economic History*, 17, 379–410.

Romer, C. (1986) 'New Estimates of Prewar GNP and Unemployment', *Journal of Economic History*, 46, 341–52.

Romer, C. (1988) 'World War I and Postwar Depression: A Reinterpretation Based on Alternative Estimates of GNP', *Journal of Monetary Economics*, 22, 91–115.

Rowe, J. W. F (1965) *Primary Commodities in International Trade*, Cambridge.

Rowthorn, R. E. and Solomou, S. N. (1991) 'The Macroeconomic Effects of Overseas Investment on the UK Balance of Trade, 1870–1913', *Economic History Review*, 44, 654–64.

Russo, J. A., Jr (1966) 'The Impact of Weather on the Construction Industry of the United States', *Bulletin of the American Meteorological Society*, 47, 967–72.

Sheffrin, S. M. (1988) 'Have Economic Fluctuations Been Dampened? A Look at Evidence Outside the United States', *Journal of Monetary Economics*, 21, 73–83.

Slutsky, E. (1937) 'The Summation of Random Causes as the Cause of Cyclical Processes', *Econometrica*, 5, 105–46.

Solomou, S. N. (1987) *Phases of Economic Growth, 1850–1973: Kondratieff Waves and Kuznets Swings*, Cambridge.

Solomou, S. N. (1994) 'Economic Fluctuations, 1870–1913', in R. Floud and D. N. McCloskey (Eds), *The Economic History of Britain Since 1700*, Vol. 2, second edition, Cambridge.

Solomou, S. N. (1996) *Themes in Macroeconomic History: The UK Economy 1919–1939*, Cambridge.

Solomou, S. N. and Catao, L. A. V. (1994) 'Real Exchange Rates During the Classical Gold Standard 1870–1913: The Core Industrial Countries', Department of Applied Economics Working Paper, No. 9403, Cambridge University.

Solomou, S. N. and Weale, M. R. (1991) 'Balanced Estimates of U.K. GDP, 1870–1913', *Explorations in Economic History*, 23, 54–63.

Solomou, S. N. and Weale, M. R. (1996) 'UK National Income 1920–38: The Implications of Balanced Estimates', *Economic History Review*, 49, 101–15.

Solomou, S. N. and Wu, W. (1998) 'Weather and Construction Sector Output Fluctuations 1860–1913', Department of Applied Economics Working Paper, Cambridge University.

Sommariva, A. and Tullio, G. (1987) *German Macroeconomic History, 1880–1979*, London.

Temin, P. (1971) 'The Beginning of the Depression in Germany', *Economic History Review*, 24, 240–8.

Temin, P. (1976) *Did Monetary Factors Cause the Great Depression?*, New York.

Temin, P. (1989) *Lessons from the Great Depression*, Cambridge, Mass.

Thomas, B. (1954) *Migration and Economic Growth*, revised edition 1973, Cambridge.

Tobin, J. (1980) *Asset Accumulation and Economic Activity: Reflections on Contemporary Macroeconomic Theory*, Chicago.

Walton, D. R. (1988) 'Does GNP Have a Unit Root? Evidence for the UK', *Economics Letters*, 26, 219–24.

Zarnowitz, V. (1981) 'Business Cycles and Growth', reprinted as chapter 7 of V. Zarnowitz (1992), *Business Cycles: Theory, History, Indicators and Forecasting*, Chicago.

Zarnowitz, V. (1985) 'Recent Work on Business Cycles in Historical Perspective: A Review of Theories and Evidence', *Journal of Economic Literature*, 23, 523–80.

Zarnowitz, V. (1992) *Business Cycles: Theory, History, Indicators and Forecasting*, Chicago.

Chapter 3

Long economic fluctuations

Introduction

The path of long-run economic growth in modern industrial economies has not been steady. The long cycle perspective emphasises the *cyclical* evolution of economic growth: long periods of high economic growth alternate with downswing phases of slow economic growth. Two long cycle frameworks have been extensively discussed in the literature on historical growth: first, the Kondratieff wave, named after the Russian economist who described the growth process of the major industrial countries as following a 50-year cycle; secondly, the Kuznets swing, named after the American economist who observed and analysed 20-year trend fluctuations in the US economy. The pattern of post-war economic growth appears to fall within the range expected from the Kondratieff wave framework, with a long boom period of rapid economic growth during 1950–73 followed by growth retardation in the two decades after 1973.[1] Two questions arise from such evidence. First, can this pattern of cyclical economic growth also be observed in the period before World War II? Secondly, if the

---

1 The choice of 1973 for the segmentation of the trend reflects the growth changes observed after the oil shock of 1973–4.

pattern is unique to the post-war era, are there mechanisms by which a similar cyclical process will be propagated in the future?

The Kuznets swing pattern of economic growth seems most pervasive during the classical gold standard period (1870–1913). This pattern of fluctuation changed significantly in the twentieth century: Abramovitz (1968) speaks of 'the passing of the Kuznets cycle' after 1913. However, as various regions of the world economy attempt to create fixed exchange rate zones and single currency areas the experience of the classical gold standard era will shed some interesting insights into the cyclical adjustment paths we expect to observe in the future. At the heart of both approaches is the idea that the demarcation line between the processes generating economic growth and business cycles is not easy to draw. The path of modern economic growth needs to be modelled as a cyclical rather than a steady or random process. Clearly, if economies are subjected to such long cyclical patterns, economic policy needs to take on a very different role to what is perceived at present. An understanding of these cyclical paths will allow us to draw out their policy implications.

This chapter describes these two cyclical frameworks and evaluates their historical relevance. The evidence is then used to discuss the implications of long cycles for the contemporary world.

Kondratieff cycles[2]

Kondratieff was one of the first economists to provide a thorough statistical analysis of cycles of prices and output with

2   The Kondratieff cycle has also been referred to as, *inter alia*, major cycle, long wave, long cycle, secular trend, secondary secular movement, secondary deviation, trend period and *mouvements de longue durée*.

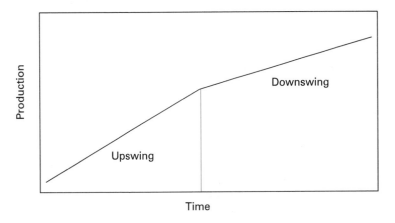

Figure 6 Kondratieff's long cycle: two-phase schema.

an average period of 50–60 years. He argued that during the period 1780–1920 the price *level* fluctuated with a 50-year cycle:[3] deflationary periods of two to three decades alternated with inflationary periods of similar duration. Prices were seen to move pro-cyclically with output growth; periods of inflation were associated with phases of rapid economic growth and periods of deflation with phases of slow economic growth. Figure 6 presents the key features of Kondratieff's schema for long cycles.

In his first study of long cycles Kondratieff (1922) referred exclusively to evidence from price movements. In later work he attempted to study long cycles as *real* phenomena affecting aggregate output. Kondratieff's 1925 study, the most well known in the English-speaking world, is mainly an empirical

---

3   Kondratieff was aware that there was a variance to the mean duration of the cycle. However, he pointed out that the variance was not large enough to invalidate the statistical significance of the cycle.

Box 2   Kondratieff's long cycle periods

First long wave:
    upswing   1780s – 1810/17
    downswing   1810/17 – 1844/51

Second long wave:
    upswing   1844/51 – 1870/75
    downswing   1870/75 – 1890/96

Third long wave:
    upswing   1890/96 – 1914/20
    downswing   1914/20 – ?

exercise to test for the existence of long fluctuations in prices and output. Ordinary least squares trend lines were fitted to per capita data to describe long-run trend movements; in order to eliminate short cycles from his analysis he then used a nine-year moving average of the deviations from trend to smooth the data. The choice of a nine-year moving average reflected the conventional wisdom in Kondratieff's time that the major industrial countries were influenced by trade cycles with an average period of nine years (often referred to as Juglar cycles). The periodisation put forward by Kondratieff from this exercise is given in Box 2.

Kondratieff's early work had little to say on the economic processes generating long waves; the emphasis was on describing their key features. Five descriptive characteristics were noted:

- during upswings of economic growth, years of prosperity are more numerous, whereas years of depression predominate during the downswing phases;

- the agricultural sector is particularly depressed during long wave downswings;
- innovations (what Kondratieff calls inventions) are assumed to cluster during the downswing phases, and their large-scale application occurs during the next long upswing;
- gold production increases during the beginning of the long upswing, and the world market for goods is enlarged by the assimilation of new countries;
- wars and revolutions tend to occur during upswing phases.

All these aspects were assumed to be part of an endogenous cyclical process rather than exogenous explanations for the existence of long waves. Even wars were seen as part of an endogenous long cycle originating from the 'increased tension of economic life, in the heightened economic struggle for markets and raw materials' (Kondratieff, 1925, p. 539 of 1979 translation). Kondratieff's cyclical theory was developed further in a paper read before the Economics Institute in Moscow in 1926. The idea that was put forward was of a 50-year investment cycle, similar to Marx's theory of the trade cycle:

> The material basis of long cycles is the wear and tear, the replacement and the increase of the fund of basic capital goods, the production of which requires tremendous investment and is a long process. (Quoted in Garvy, 1943, p. 208)

Kondratieff's methodology has been subject to a number of important criticisms, which have forced the debate over long waves to evolve to integrate new evidence and a more theoretical structure. First, a concentration on price history can be very misleading as an indicator of production trends; the relationship between long-run price and output movements has not proved to be stable over time. For example, in the British case the deflationary periods of 1820–50 and 1873–96 were associated with higher or comparable growth rates to the inflationary periods of 1850–73 and 1896–1913 (Crafts, 1985; Matthews *et al.*, 1982; Solomou, 1987; Williamson, 1984). Secondly, the waves are supposed to reflect the development path of the capitalist world economy:

> The long waves that we have established above relating to the series most important in economic life are international; and the timing of these cycles corresponds fairly well for European capitalistic countries. (Kondratieff, 1925, p. 535 of 1979 translation)

However, the available evidence suggests that countries were not growing along synchronised paths before 1920. The inverse growth phases between Europe and the US have been well documented (Thomas, 1973). The early twentieth century was an upswing phase of economic growth in many newly industrialising countries and a period of slow economic growth in Britain: since nations were not at a similar stage of economic development, growth opportunities differed significantly across countries. Hence, investment funds did not remain idle during depressed phases in the leading economies (as implied by Kondratieff) but flowed to regions with a relatively higher rate of return, reflecting a potential for high economic growth. The inverse pattern between British home and overseas investment has been widely noted (Cairncross, 1953; Edelstein, 1982). Such a pattern has also been observed for France and Germany (Solomou, 1987). Hence, the *closed* economic system assumed by Kondratieff to represent the pre-1920 world economy offers a misleading perspective: the era was one of differing growth opportunities across countries. Kondratieff did recognise that the US was in many ways out of line with some of his evidence but he did not stress the full implications of this observation within a world economy perspective. Economic growth during the period that Kondratieff analysed was neither balanced (whereby every country grows at the same rate) nor synchronised across countries.

Schumpeter (1939) diffused Kondratieff's ideas in the English-speaking world and refined the explanatory framework. He saw long cycles as resulting from the effects of lumpy, long gestation investments. Such investment was made possible by clusters of major innovations, such as railway and electricity networks. Many recent studies have developed Schumpeter's theory of long waves by linking the concept of product life cycles to the Schumpeterian idea of innovation clusters. For example, Mensch (1979) provides a modern restatement of Schumpeter's ideas. Mensch describes economic growth as being characterised by a series of intermittent innovative impulses that take the form of **'S'-shaped growth trajectories**. He postulates a *metamorphosis model*, depicting long periods of stable economic growth and relatively shorter intervals of economic turbulence. He begins with the following working hypothesis of basic innovations:

> A technological event is a technological basic innovation when the newly discovered material or newly developed technique is being put into regular production for the first time, or when an organised market for the new product is first created. (Mensch, 1979, p. 123)

He argues that there is only limited interest in implementing basic innovation during prosperous phases of growth; in such periods only minor improvements are introduced. In contrast, during major depression phases, when the old technologies have outlived their usefulness in sustaining profitability and economic growth, there is greater pressure to introduce basic innovations, induced by low profit rates on the old technology and high potential profitability on new technology.

The empirical validity of Mensch's framework is dependent on proving the existence of *regular recurring* clusters in basic innovations.[4] Mensch rationalises innovation clusters in terms of the pressures on profitability during major depressions. However, without assuming the long wave pattern of major depressions as a macroeconomic conditioning factor, it is difficult to see why basic innovations should cluster in the interval of regular 50-year long cycles. The explanation for regular clusters has remained a major theoretical problem in the long wave literature (Garvy, 1943; Kuznets, 1940; Rosenberg and Frischtak, 1983). Some of the empirical aspects relating to long wave clusters are considered below.

Not all the literature has viewed long waves as *real* fluctuations in the macroeconomy: for example, both Rostow and Kennedy (1979) and Lewis (1978) have argued that the Kondratieff wave is best seen only as a *price* phenomenon that has its roots in a series of sectoral imbalances in the world economy. Given long lags for returns on investment in the production of primary commodities, it proves difficult to produce or sustain an equilibrium level of output where supply equals demand: as a result, the primary producing sector suffers from long periods of disequilibrium. An overproduction of primary commodities will give rise to an adverse movement of the terms of trade for the sector, which will reduce the price level and raise the real wage level of industrial economies. The

---

4   Moreover, even if product life cycles cluster at a point in time, life cycles should correspond at all points in time for a long wave to arise in the aggregate growth path of the economy.

adverse movement of the terms of trade against primary producers will depress exports from industrial countries, but the higher real wage in the industrial sectors (countries) means that domestic demand may compensate for the fall in export demand. Hence, retarded aggregate economic growth is not a necessary feature of Kondratieff cycles: long cycles are primarily reflected in prices, relative prices and sectoral real variables.

Kuznets swings

Abramovitz has defined such movements as:

> swings in the level or rate of growth of a variable with a duration longer than the normal business cycles but shorter than the very long swings with which Kondratieff, Schumpeter and others have been concerned. To permit ample room to consider all the possible relevant evidence, we might set the minimum at five years and the maximum at thirty. (Quoted in Easterlin, 1968, p. 6)

The length of the swings found in the empirical literature has varied: Kuznets (1958), Abramovitz (1959) and Lewis and O'Leary (1955) found mean durations for these swings of 22, 14 and 19 years, respectively. The different durations are the result of different smoothing and trend elimination techniques (Bird *et al.*, 1965), but the *existence* of the swings is not critically dependent on the employment of these techniques. Many economic series display Kuznets swings in the untransformed data.

Kuznets swings have often been explained within monocausal frameworks emphasising the Anglo-American evidence. Cairncross (1953) explained long swings in terms of the relative overproduction between manufactures and primary commodities in the world economy; Thomas (1954) explained the Anglo-American swings in terms of the exogenous effects of large migration movements across the Atlantic, inducing multi-plier-accelerator effects of an inverse type in Britain and the US. More recently explanations have favoured models emphasising an endogenous interaction of economic–demographic variables (Abramovitz, 1961; Easterlin, 1968; Hickman, 1974; Kuznets, 1958). The model presented in Figure 7 captures the key features of this perspective. Instead of assuming a simple investment–income relationship (the **accelerator theory**) the long swing literature emphasises that rapid growth of incomes increases labour supply (via migration flows); since migrants tend to cluster in the working age group, family formation increases, giving strong stimulus to population-sensitive invest-ments, such as building and construction. In these approaches migration is not an exogenous variable that generates long swings; instead it is part of the feedback mechanisms generat-ing long swings by affecting the adjustment lags in the economic system.

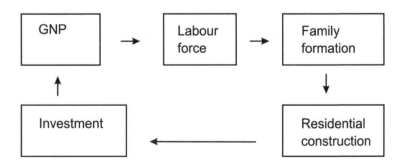

Figure 7   Economic–demographic Kuznets swing model.

Long swings have been observed in a wide variety of variables, including GDP, balance of payments, productivity, money supply, investment, sectoral terms of trade, and agricultural output, in addition to migration (Solomou, 1987). The evidence also suggests that long swings are observed in a wide variety of countries during 1870–1913, including Germany (Metz and Spree, 1981; Solomou, 1987), France (Lévy-Leboyer, 1978; Solomou, 1987), Canada (Harkness, 1968), Brazil (Catao, 1991), Argentina (Ford, 1974), Australia (Pope, 1984) and Japan (Minami, 1986; Ohkawa and Rosovsky, 1973). It would seem that existing theories have overemphasised the Anglo-American economic–demographic causal mechanisms to the neglect of other important influences.

Empirical analyses of Kondratieff cycles

Most economists find the empirical evidence for Kondratieff cycles to be weak. Garvy (1943) concluded that the waves identified by Kondratieff are, in part at least, statistical artefacts resulting from the techniques he employed to analyse long-run time-series data. Lewis (1978) concluded that long waves in production are not observed for the four major industrial economies (Britain, France, Germany and the US) or for the weighted sum of these economies (often referred to as the *core* economies). Using spectral analysis (a statistical technique for analysing the existence of cycles of different durations) Van Ewijk (1981) found no evidence for the existence of a Kondratieff cycle in aggregate production. Beenstock (1983) examined Kondratieff's original data with the technique of spectral analysis and found no evidence of long cycles in either nominal or real variables.

Van Duijn (1983) and Kleinknecht (1987) have argued a case for the existence of Kondratieff waves. Van Duijn found that although the evidence for long cycles is weak when we examine the growth path of individual countries, there is stronger evidence for long cycles in the growth path of the world economy. In this section I will survey the recent empirical research focusing on national and world economy trends.

Long cycles in national economic growth

The focus of recent research has been on the major industrial countries (Britain, France, Germany and the US). In the case of the Britain, most studies fail to find a pattern of Kondratieff long waves since 1850. Matthews *et al.* (1982) recognise that British economic growth has shown long-run variations but do not observe Kondratieff cycles. The pattern of long-run growth is depicted in Figure 8.[5] Clearly, a Kondratieff cyclical pattern has not been observed. Others (Kleinknecht, 1987; Solomou, 1987; Van Duijn, 1983) have found a similar result.

Some recent work has tried to rehabilitate the relevance of Kondratieff cycles in the British economy (Metz, 1992; Reijnders, 1992). However, these studies rely on statistical methods that are problematic. For example, Metz's result holds only if we interpolate data for the world wars; he finds that including the wars in the sample reduces the period of the cycle significantly. Reijnders argues that in order to correct for what he calls

5   The slowdown of British economic growth during 1899–1913 has not
     been found to be significant in a number of more recent studies. Using
     the Kalman filter to estimate the trend movement of the pre-1914
     British economy Crafts *et al.* (1989) depict the long-run growth path
     as being steady over the period 1856–1913. This does not rule out a
     cyclical retardation of trend growth during the period 1899–1913.

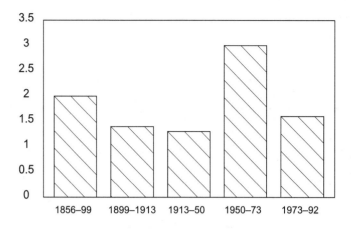

Figure 8 British GDP (percentage long-term compound growth rate).

perspectivistic distortion, which arises as a general problem because time-series of different lengths manifest different trend movements, we need to consider very long-run time-series to get a corrected perception of the underlying trend. He uses the Phelps-Brown and Hopkins price series, which covers 690 years to standardise the long-run trend. In following this procedure very unreliable price data are used to describe the output trend behaviour of modern industrial economies. Long-run time-series contain useful information only if the data are reliable and relevant to a particular economic structure. We cannot overcome the problem that the only reliable *annual* macroeconomic data we have are from the second half of the nineteenth century[6] onwards (and even they have a high measurement error).

6   One way to increase our quantitative information set is to pool time-series and cross-sectional data since 1850. For example, Maddison's (1991) data set for 16 countries is useful in this respect.

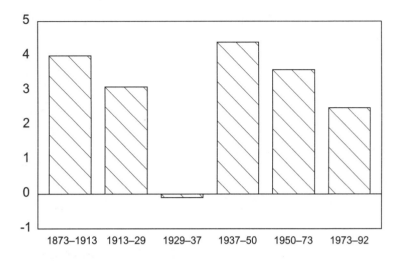

Figure 9   US GDP (percentage long-term compound growth rate).

Most studies have also failed to find evidence of Kondratieff cycles in the production trends of the US economy. Lewis (1978) focused on the period 1870–1913 and failed to find a long wave in industrial production. Solomou (1987) analysed data for the period 1870–1973 and failed to find a Kondratieff cycle pattern in GDP growth: the most significant long-run growth variations were associated with the growth stagnation of the 1930s and the resurgence of growth in the 1940s. Studies that have used the Kondratieff cycle to model the path of US economic growth have done so under restrictive assumptions: Bieshaar and Kleinknecht (1986) argue that a Kondratieff cycle pattern describes US economic growth after 1890. As can be seen in Figure 9, a fast growth phase during 1890–1913 or 1890–1929 gives way to stagnation in the 1930s and is followed by a strong revival of economic growth after 1940. Metz (1992) also found a Kondratieff cycle pattern over 1889–

1979; however, this result is dependent on excluding the world war shocks and neglecting the available evidence for the 1870s and 1880s; including the war years, the period of the long cycle is reduced significantly. Given the importance of historical shocks to the growth process, it is difficult to justify a procedure that interpolates the war years. Similarly, neglecting the information on the 1870s and 1880s leads to a distorted picture of the US growth during 1870–1913. Considering both pieces of information results in the conventional picture that the US economy manifested a Kuznets swing growth process (and not a Kondratieff wave) both during the classical gold standard period (Abramovitz, 1968) and since 1913 (Hickman, 1974; Solomou, 1987).

The German case has proved particularly difficult to analyse given problems of data reliability. German macro-economic data are based on the work of Hoffmann (1965). But Hoffmann's macroeconomic data pose serious problems for the period 1870–84, which has proved to be important in long cycle discussions (Lewis, 1978, 1981). Hoffmann's output data are mainly derived from trade data. However, the basis of recording German imports changed several times during this period, the biggest change occurring in 1879. For example, between 1872 and 1879 the transit trade is included (but not always) in import statistics but not fully in export statistics. Published import figures show a fall of 25 per cent between 1879 and 1880 and Hoffmann translated this into a constant price fall of 24 per cent. But independent evidence on the performance of the economy shows that 1880 is, in fact, a prosperous year. Hoffmann's index of manufacturing (excluding construction and mining) fell 3 per cent over 1879–80; during the same period his indices for minerals, metal production and railway traffic rose by 12 per cent, 16 per cent and 13 per cent, respectively (representing series that were not affected by customs statistics). Thus, the severity and length of the depression of 1874–84 are clearly overstated by Hoffmann, which affects our perception of German long cycles throughout 1870–1914.

Lewis (1978) has gone further, arguing that the severe and long depression of the 1870s is *purely* a product of Hoffmann's inappropriate data construction methods rather than a description of the true path of the German economy. To arrive at this conclusion Lewis notes that an index of German coal production grew at the same rate as the index of manufacturing between 1884 and 1913 and also between 1866 and 1871. He then substituted the coal production index over the years 1871–84 for Hoffmann's manufacturing index between those dates. The industrial production index constructed by Lewis for the period 1865–1913 shows steady growth (with a short trade cycle) during 1873–1913. The long phase of depression during the 1870s is noted only by its absence.

However, it is likely that Lewis's revisions to Hoffmann's data have generated the statistical artefact of steady growth (Solomou, 1987). Although Lewis is correct in noting that manufacturing and coal production grew at the same mean rate from 1866 to 1873 and from 1884 to 1913, they did not do so before 1866. Moreover, although the two indices *averaged* the same growth rate over the period 1884–1913 the time paths of the growth variations were quite different. In fact, since Lewis is in effect using coal production as an *indicator variable* for aggregate industrial production, it would be more efficient (in a statistical sense) to employ this index throughout its availability; using it only for the period 1871–84 makes it an arbitrary proxy. In contrast to Lewis's conclusion, the time path of coal production shows a period of slow growth during 1873–91

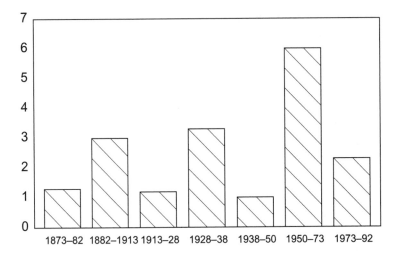

Figure 10   German GDP (percentage long-term compound growth rate).

relative to 1857–73 and 1891–1913 (Solomou, 1987). As a proxy for the growth performance of the industrial sector, this series clearly shows a phase of retarded economic growth during the 1870s and the early 1880s. No doubt much of the *severity* of the depression of the 1870s is an artefact resulting from Hoffmann's use of import data to calculate production indices. Nevertheless, Lewis has drawn strong inferences from arbitrary assumptions. Figure 10 presents a summary of the macroeconomic trends in the light of this discussion. Clearly, there have been long-run growth shifts: long boom periods have given way to periods of growth retardation. However, the periods of growth retardation have been short and, in general, have been associated with war shocks and adjustments such as 1913–28 and 1938–50. Metz (1992) found that when the war years are included in the statistical analysis the time path of the

German growth swings is in the time domain of Kuznets swings rather than the Kondratieff cycle.

Long cycles in world economic growth

Jaap Van Duijn has argued that long waves of economic growth are best seen as a feature of the world economy rather than nation states:

> Great Britain, the USA, Germany and France each have their own histories, in which the S-shaped life cycle of economic development may be more conspicuous than long wave fluctuations. The industrialized world as a whole, or even the four core countries taken together, moves forward along a long wave path. (Van Duijn, 1983, p. 154)

The production trends of the world economy provide some support for this view. The long-run growth pattern in Maddison's world GDP series (a weighted average of 16 countries) (Maddison, 1982, 1991; Solomou, 1987) is depicted in Figure 11. The pattern of long-run growth variations since 1870 suggest variations of the Kondratieff duration. World exports show a similar pattern to world production trends (Lewis, 1981). It is important to emphasise, however, that this evidence cannot *prove* the existence of a propagation mechanism that generates long cycles as an endogenous economic outcome. A number of shocks have played an important role in generating the phases of upswing and downswing in world economic performance. Solomou (1986a) accounts for the upswing in world economic growth during 1890–1913 with two main influences. First, countries were growing at differential rates during 1870–1913. Thus, while GDP in Britain and France grew at 2 per cent or less, the German rate averaged 3 per cent

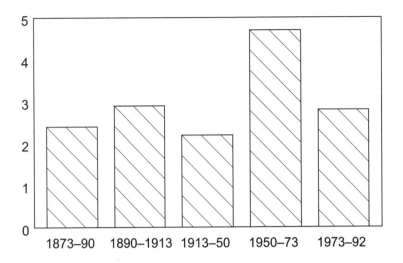

Figure 11 World economy (16 major countries) (percentage long-term compound growth rate).

and the US rate 4 per cent. As the weight of the fast-growing economies increased over time, the world economy saw a stepping up of long-run economic growth. Secondly, many smaller countries started growing at an expanding rate after 1890. Thus, to understand the upswing of 1890–1913 we need to understand why countries industrialise when they do, rather than why economic growth follows a long cycle. Both these effects are outcomes of one-off historical processes rather than being part of a cyclical structure in world economic growth.

The break in long-run economic growth during 1913–38 can partly be seen as the outcome of these long-run structural changes and the instabilities they gave rise to. For example, the transition to US leadership of the world economy between 1890 and the 1920s also transferred many of the instabilities of US economic growth to the world economy (Kindleberger, 1983). Throughout the period 1870–1913 the volatility of US

economic growth was much greater than that of the major
industrial European economies. The US had a financial and
credit structure that was prone to the effects of financial
fragility (Minsky, 1964). The 1930s depression was one such
event. Moreover, the transition in world economic leadership
was associated with the failure of world institutions (such as
the gold standard) to stabilise the international economy
(Eichengreen, 1992).

The 'cycle' of upswing after World War II is partly the
outcome of major institutional changes and a catching-up
process that was made possible by the relative backwardness of
the European economies. World War II had widened the large
gap between the productivity levels of the US and Europe.
Given that the institutional changes were partly the outcome of
the policy lessons drawn from the experiences of the inter-war
period, there are important cyclical influences on the long-run
path of economies. The cyclical aspect of this path (which is
neither regular nor periodic) seems to arise from developments
in the institutional structure of the world economy. Given the
slow evolution of international institutions, the world economy
has frequently seen international coordination failures. However, in the long run, the institutions of the world economy
have evolved via learning. Thus the policy lessons of the inter-
war era led to the formation of a new world order after World
War II that reacted to some of the problems of the previous
period. What is clear, however, is that the evolution of new
institutions is not predetermined. A number of outcomes are
possible and each of these outcomes will yield different growth
effects on the world economy or particular regions of the world
economy. The time path for the evolution of new institutions is
also not predetermined. Although the observed fluctuations in
world economic performance seem to follow a Kondratieff

cycle, the small sample of observations since 1870 means that this specific period could easily be the outcome of chance.

Innovation clusters

The long wave perspective to innovation, as seen by Kondratieff and Schumpeter, specifies the existence of *regular* clusters at approximately 50–60-year intervals. Since the innovation data available cover only a few complete waves we cannot analyse the existence of *cycles* as such. Nevertheless, there remains the possibility of testing a weak Kondratieff wave hypothesis that *episodic* historical waves of 50–60-year periodicity may have existed.

A starting point in this discussion is the empirical work of Mensch (1979). From a list of 127 basic innovations between 1740 and 1955 Mensch postulated that basic innovations have

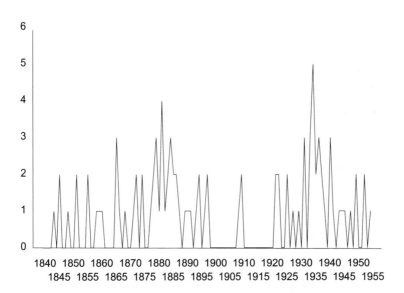

Figure 12   Numbers of basic innovations over time (Mensch selection).

clustered during long wave depression phases. The major depressions are taken from Kuznets' periodisation of long wave depression phases (Kuznets, 1930, 1940). Mensch postulated basic innovation clusters during three major depressions:

- 1813–27
- 1871–85
- 1926–38

In fact, from Figure 12 there is a *prima facie* case for the existence of innovation clusters during these phases. He found that irrespective of the periodisation scheme, the likelihood that the observed discontinuities were simply the work of a random process was well under the 5 per cent significance level. Thus, the null hypothesis postulating randomness was rejected[7] and Mensch concluded: 'The consistent pattern of ups and downs in the innovation stream must therefore be treated as an assured empirical fact' (1979, p. 134).

Freeman *et al.* (1982, pp. 57–64) have provided extensive evidence criticising Mensch's sampling methods for the twentieth century. Given that Mensch (1979) draws a distinction between major (basic) and minor innovation there are problems in defining the innovation population. Even if agreement is reached that basic innovation is a meaningful concept, a weighting structure for these innovations is needed. More important, perhaps, is the fact that by its very nature innovation cannot be treated in mechanistic terms; the considerations

7   Mensch tested for statistical significance by considering whether the pattern of innovations in the sample could have been generated by a random process. He examines this using non-parametric runs tests on the data based on 1-year, 2-year, 3-year, ... 10-year classifications.

for introducing major and minor innovations cannot differ greatly. It is only *ex post* that some innovations can be said to have had a greater impact than others. Such problems imply that the population of basic innovations is undefined. Without knowledge of the population Mensch cannot claim to have a random sampling procedure; instead he has a *selection* procedure from an unknown population. The biases in the selection procedure are manifested in the technological bias of his basic innovation listing. Mensch's analysis of innovation lacks Schumpeter's commercial and organisational orientation to innovation.

As an example of the kinds of biases involved in Mensch's selection procedure, consider his twentieth-century data (Freeman *et al.*, 1982, pp. 44–57). Mensch takes most of his innovations from Jewkes *et al.* (1969). But Jewkes *et al.* never claimed that their selection of 60 inventions in the first edition (or 70 in the second) was in any sense complete or a random sample. Since Mensch relies mainly on the first edition, his study could not do justice to the innovations of the 1950s. Mensch also omits 20 inventions from Jewkes *et al.*'s list (30 from the second edition) and almost all of these fall outside the cluster of the 1930s. Moreover, while Jewkes *et al.* were concerned with invention Mensch was concerned with innovation. Hence, Mensch fails to have a representative sample of innovations in the early twentieth century – for 1900–20 Mensch's sample contains only three innovations.

Consistency in the sample is also not examined by Mensch. The innovations in the sample will be comparable over time only if the factors determining the propensity to innovate are unchanged over time. A key influence on the propensity to innovate was noted by Schumpeter, who argued that large monopolistic firms have more incentive to produce inventions

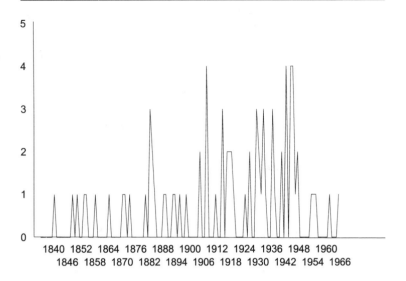

Figure 13   Number of basic innovations over time (Van Duijn selection).

and innovate because they can more easily appropriate the benefits (Schumpeter, 1950, chapters 7 and 8). Given the changed market structures between the nineteenth and twentieth centuries, long-run innovation series are not strictly comparable. In addition, the research and development sector has grown rapidly since the 1920s, suggesting a structural shift relative to the nineteenth century.

As a way of overcoming some of the sampling problems Solomou (1986b) undertook a test of Mensch's thesis employing Van Duijn's (1983, p. 181) more extensive and representative innovation selection for the period 1870–1950 (see Figure 13). Employing Van Duijn's selection leaves little of Mensch's hypothesis of a clustering of innovations during major depression phases. Innovation flows have not displayed depression-induced clusters.[8] The only major disturbance arises from the world wars. The differing effects of World War I from those of World War II can mainly be understood in terms of the technological differences between them.

Summarising, it is clear that although the innovation flow has been subjected to a number of major shocks and structural discontinuities, a regular long cycle has not been observed. Given the central role of technical change to the growth process, such discontinuities are expected to have an impact on the path of long-run economic growth. However, the expected effect is to generate a random walk or segmented trends in output levels rather than a long cycle of the Kondratieff type.

Empirical analyses of Kuznets swings

During 1870–1913 long swings, approximately 20 years in duration, were a pervasive feature of national economic growth. Such swings were observed in both the major industrial countries and a number of primary producing countries. For example, US productivity and output growth fluctuated with large long swing variations during 1873–1912. Similar swings are also observed in construction, investment and monetary growth (Abramovitz, 1961; Friedman and Schwartz, 1982).[9] The French experience also suggests the relevance of

8 Van Duijn (1983, p. 182) reports the following innovation flows: 1872–92 = 24; 1892–1913 = 23; 1913–29 = 11; 1929–48 = 38.
9 Although Romer (1986) has raised doubts about the reliability of Kuznets' data, her concerns focus on measures of variance; the mean long-term and medium-term growth path of the Kuznets' data remain unchanged. Moreover, a reduced variance in the pre-1909 data has the effect of raising the statistical significance of long swing growth fluctuations in the US economy (Solomou, 1987).

Kuznets swings in the pre-1914 era. Lévy-Leboyer's (1978) series for commodity production (a weighted average of agricultural and industrial output) shows a marked long swing growth pattern during 1869–1913. He also notes the importance of the 20-year investment cycle in the French economy with even greater inter-period growth variations than were observed in commodity production. The productivity and output growth performance of Germany and Britain can also be depicted as a long swing process during 1870–1913 (Solomou, 1987). The strongest evidence for a long swing pattern of growth is to be found in less aggregated variables. Domestic and overseas investment, money supply growth, the balance of trade, migration, all show irregular and significant long swing trend variations.

Long swings have often been explained as the outcome of the pre-1914 economic structure, with population-sensitive investments having a central role. The emphasis has been on the Anglo-American economies, with the aim of explaining the economic impact of international migration movements. Kuznets (1958) suggested that internal and international migration responded to development opportunities in the US economy, inducing multiplier-accelerator effects via the building sector. Abramovitz (1959, 1961) and Easterlin (1968) have offered similar explanations.

Working within the migration perspective, Thomas (1954) attempted to explain migration and aggregate long swings in terms of the framework of the Atlantic economy. In Thomas's early work the Atlantic economy consisted of Britain and the US; in later work it consists of the 'core' and 'periphery' economies (Thomas, 1973). The high degree of economic integration in the Atlantic economy implies that the availability of factors of production was a constraint on economic growth within the region. An increase of investment in one region was assumed to result in a decrease of investment in the other. Since construction was greatly influenced by population changes, which, in turn, were influenced by migration movements, migration was the main force generating swings in output and investment. These swings would be inverse for the different regions of the Atlantic economy.

That *exogenous* migration swings can generate macro-economic swings is theoretically plausible (Parry-Lewis, 1964). However, exogeneity needs to be justified, as does the monocausal framework. To the extent that migration patterns are influenced by economic considerations, Thomas's (1954) model is misleading; the description of endogenous economic processes has been confused with an exogenous explanation of economic change. Moreover, the emphasis on migration as the *causal* variable has led to a neglect of other important influences on long swings.

Cairncross (1953) focused on the variation of the sectoral terms of trade between manufactures and agriculture in the world economy. Britain, France and Germany were representative of industrial economies producing manufactured commodities while much of the rest of the world was taken to represent the primary producing sector. Investment flows in the international economy were determined by the relative profitability of these two sectors. Migration flows were not an exogenous force generating long swings but were merely responding to these underlying economic variations. In Cairncross's framework changes in the sectoral terms of trade reflected long-run sectoral imbalances in the world economy:

One would expect to find, therefore, that during, or immediately after, a fairly long period in which the terms of trade were relatively unfavourable to Britain there would be heavy investment in the countries supplying her with imports.... On the other hand, when capital goods were expensive and foodstuffs were in over-supply, the continuance of a rapid opening up of agricultural countries would be distinctly surprising. (Cairncross, 1953, p. 189)

Cairncross argued that a similar experience is also observed for the other major capital exporters.

All these early studies of pre-1914 long swings emphasise monocausality, partly because of the limited macroeconomic and sectoral data available to the early researchers. As noted above, long swings were observed for, *inter alia*, aggregate investment, profitability, output, productivity, agricultural output, construction output, weather variables, monetary growth, sectoral terms of trade and migration flows. The swings also have international dimensions: they are observed for overseas investment, the international terms of trade and international relative profitability movements and the balance of trade. Such evidence raises strong doubts about the simple migration and terms of trade explanations for these swings.

Research into long swings has generally been limited to studies of the pre-1914 era. Abramovitz (1968) argued that Kuznets swings were a feature only of the pre-1914 era, partly because the introduction of migration restrictions in the New World during the inter-war period changed the causal processes behind the swings. Moreover, given the long boom in most OECD economies after 1945 the idea of 20-year growth swings seemed anachronous. However, in arguing the case for 'the passing of the Kuznets cycle' Abramovitz is relying on the validity of the prior hypothesis that growth swings of this duration were the outcome of *international* migration swings. In the US economy *domestic* migration swings were equally important after 1914 (Easterlin, 1968; Hickman, 1963). Thus, the US economy saw a long swing pattern of macroeconomic growth continue into the inter-war and post-war eras (Hickman, 1974).

One neglected area of research is the importance of policy regimes in creating an institutional structure that allows long swings to arise as part of the cyclical adjustment process. It is now well recognised that the French growth experience during the 1930s is partly explained by a commitment to the gold standard and the deflationary policy regime this imposed (Eichengreen, 1992). A similar experience was observed in all the gold bloc economies (France, Belgium, Italy, Poland and Switzerland) during the 1930s. The interesting question that arises from this is whether the gold standard policy regime was a common feature conditioning the adjustment path to shocks before 1914. The pervasiveness of long swings before 1914 suggests that this is a possibility that needs further research. The pervasive nature of Kuznets swings before 1914 suggests that such growth variations are best seen as aspects of the international adjustment mechanism of the era, conditioned by two key features of the period. First, the rules-driven policy framework implied that national policy had to be used to defend the credibility of the gold standard, giving governments limited national policy options. Secondly, free capital and labour flows across countries generated cyclical adjustment to shocks. In chapter 2 we noted that this resulted in inverse trend movements between exports, investment and consumption in the leading industrial countries.

The key change during the inter-war period was the passing of the international adjustment aspects of long swings. National policy regimes shifted over short periods, introducing more discretionary policy responses to shocks. Migration restrictions

imposed by the New World ended the endogenous international adjustment to shocks: instead of resulting in a series
of long duration cyclical adjustments we observe the new
phenomenon of persistence in macroeconomic variables.
Adverse shocks resulted in mass unemployment rather than
mass migration.

The rebirth of long swings?

One theme that runs through this survey of economic cycles is
that institutional changes have a major effect in determining
the nature of economic cycles in different epochs. On a
speculative note I will evaluate whether long swings are a likely
outcome of proposed institutional changes, such as European
economic and monetary union (EMU). As different regions of
the world economy seek to establish fixed exchange rates and
common currencies, migration and capital flows will have to
take on a more important role in future cyclical adjustment
paths. The approach of this section is to consider a number of
scenarios that are possible under EMU.

EMU with limited adjustment mechanisms
The theory of optimum currency areas (OCA) suggests that for
Europe to function as an OCA the member countries need to
generate viable adjustment mechanisms to asymmetric shocks.
Three types of adjustment could play a key role in responding
to asymmetric shocks: fiscal transfers from central fiscal bodies
to the affected area; labour mobility, allowing workers to
emigrate from adversely affected countries; and capital mobility, which may allow depressed areas to utilise human capital.
One conditional prediction we can make is that given the

current low levels of labour and capital mobility across Europe and the limited fiscal policy aspects of EMU, asymmetric shocks are *unlikely* to result in significant adjustment. The historical analogy that comes to mind is that the Europe of the early twenty-first century will have similarities with the observed cyclical structures of the inter-war period. Adverse national-specific shocks are likely to lead to strong persistence mechanisms.

Such an institutional structure, combined with the probability of major adverse national-specific shocks, is likely to result in the persistent economic decline of particular nations, which in the long run can only threaten the political stability of EMU. In these circumstances business cycle volatility is likely to increase if political instabilities result in major policy regime changes.

EMU *with adjustment mechanisms*

The pessimistic scenario described above needs to be balanced with an outline of an economic system that is capable of generating greater degrees of adjustment. The previous conditional prediction was based on historical trends for labour and capital mobility in Europe. History cannot predict future trends. The new institutions may lead to significant changes in endogenous variables such as migration and capital flows. As a thought experiment on the future of economic cycles, let us assume that the Europe of the twenty-first century is successful in generating the required levels of labour and capital mobility to make EMU a sustainable economic institution.

If adjustment to national-specific shocks arises mainly from labour mobility, we need to evaluate the cyclical effects of such an adjustment mechanism. What this is likely to generate is the rebirth of long swing phenomena in a different form. Instead of being a feature of the world economy (as in the gold standard era) it is likely to be a feature of integrated regions, such as Europe under EMU.

Adjusting to national-specific shocks via migration creates longer lags in the economic system. Migration is likely to entail psychological, recognition and decision lags. Distinguishing a permanent from a transitory shock may be difficult and given the economic and social costs of migration, the decision process will not be instantaneous. What is being activated is a slow adjustment mechanism that will result in economic–demographic effects on business cycles. Migration will solve the unemployment problem of adversely affected countries but will also result in inverse aggregate demand effects on the sending and receiving countries. The new lagged effects being activated will result in a shift of cyclical behaviour in the economic system. A long swing is likely to arise across the different countries of Europe. Simulation results by Forrester (1977) illustrate how such lags lengthen the cyclical period.

Ex ante we cannot predict which path is the most likely, but a conditional prediction we can make is that if EMU is going to survive in the decades to come it will have to be associated with different cyclical adjustment mechanisms than have been observed in the past. In fact, the policy implication from this analysis is that supply-side policies will have to encourage cyclical adjustment by encouraging the mobility of factors of production.

Lessons and conclusions

This overview of long cycle perspectives suggests that the answers to the following two questions are quite different:

- Do regular (deterministic) long cycles exist?
- Do irregular (stochastic) long duration fluctuations exist?

The answer to the first question is clearly negative: neither Kondratieff waves nor Kuznets swings are a regular recurring feature of modern economies in the nineteenth and twentieth centuries. However, the second question is far more interesting than the first: in the light of the evidence presented above, *irregular* long duration fluctuations have been observed in modern economies. A long cycle perspective on modern economic growth helps us to understand historical paths and to think about the possible outcomes in the future. We have observed two types of long duration fluctuation. First is a long cycle in the performance of world trade and production since 1870. This is not equivalent to arguing that endogenous Kondratieff waves describe world economic development: however, a series of impulses to world institutions have propagated a cyclical pattern to world economic growth. Secondly, an irregular long duration cycle has been observed at the national level. The duration of national cycles was within a Kuznets swing time band during 1870–1914; during the inter-war period these fluctuations changed, reflecting changes in international adjustment mechanisms.

What are the propagation mechanisms and shocks generating this type of growth fluctuation? In the context of the world economy I have emphasised shocks to international institutions. In the context of Kuznets swings the emphasis has been on the implications of the type of adjustment mechanisms that were possible in the pre-1914 era. A fixed exchange rate regime imposed a rules-driven policy framework on participants, constraining the response to national-specific shocks. Such a policy stance created the need for deflation as a means of adjusting to shocks. High levels of international labour and capital mobility helped the adjustment path by reducing the required level of deflation.

As different trading and policy blocs attempt to re-establish fixed exchange rate regimes and single currency areas in the 1990s, the adjustment to shocks in the future will once again become policy constrained. For example, Europe's commitment to a single currency under EMU must imply that a number of adjustment mechanisms (such as migration and capital flows) will be activated as equilibrating mechanisms to national-specific shocks if we are not to observe persistent divergence across countries. Such flows could generate economic–demographic interactions with the cyclical process, which has clear homologies with the gold standard pattern of international adjustments. The arguments presented suggest that there exists the *possibility* of a rebirth of long swing phenomena in the future. Moreover, for a successful regionalisation of the world economy, regional and national policy makers need to pursue a policy stance that creates long duration cyclical adjustments rather than persistence. The lessons of the past point to the fact that the gold standard survived for so long partly because of the existence of historically specific adjustment mechanisms.

Bibliography

Abramovitz, M. (1959) 'Historical and Comparative Rates of Production, Productivity and Prices', Statement in US Congress, Joint Economic Committee, *Employment, Growth and Price Levels, Hearings* (86th Congress, Part II), Washington, 411–66.

Abramovitz, M. (1961) 'The Nature and Significance of Kuznets Cycles', *Economic Development and Cultural Change*, 9, 225–49.

Abramovitz, M. (1968) 'The Passing of the Kuznets Cycle', *Economica*, 35, 349–67.

Beenstock, M. (1983) *The World Economy in Transition*, London.

Bieshaar, H. and Kleinknecht, A. (1986) 'Kondratieff Long Waves in Aggregate Output? An Econometric Test', *Konjunkturpolitik*, 30, 279–303.

Bird, R. C., Desai, M. J., Enzler, J. J. and Taubman, P. J. (1965) 'Kuznets Cycles in Growth Rates: The Meaning', *International Economic Review*, 6, 229–39.

Bloomfield, A. I. (1968) *Pattern of Fluctuation in International Investment Before 1914*, Princeton Studies in International Finance, No. 21, Princeton.

Cairncross, A. K. (1953) *Home and Foreign Investment, 1870–1913: Studies in Capital Accumulation*, Cambridge.

Catao, L. A. V. (1991) 'The Transmission of Long Cycles Between Core and Periphery Economies: A Case Study of Brazil and Mexico', PhD dissertation, Cambridge University.

Crafts, N. F. R. (1985) *British Economic Growth During the Industrial Revolution*, Oxford.

Crafts, N. F. R., Leybourne, S. J. and Mills, T. C. (1989) 'The Climacteric in Late Victorian Britain and France: A Reappraisal of Evidence', *Journal of Applied Econometrics*, 4, 103–18.

Derksen, J. B. D. (1940) 'Long Cycles in Residential Building: An Explanation', *Econometrica*, 8, 97–116.

DeWolff, S. (1924) 'Prosperitats und Depressionsperioden', in O. Jensen (Ed.), *Der lebendige Marxismus: Festgabe zum 70 Geburtstage von Karl Kautsky*, Jena.

Dowling, J. and Poulson, B. W. (1974) 'Long Swings in the US Economy: A Spectral Analysis of 19th and 20th Century Data', *Southern Economic Journal*, 40, 473–80.

Dupriez, L. H. (1978) '1974: A Downturn of the Long Wave?', *Banca Nationale Del Lavoro Quarterly Review*, 126, 199–210.

Easterlin, R. A. (1966) 'Economic–Demographic Interactions and Long Swings in Economic Growth', *American Economic Review*, 56, 1063–104.

Easterlin, R. (1968) *Population, Labor Force and Long Swings in Economic Growth: The American Experience*, New York.

Edelstein, M. (1982) *Overseas Investment in the Age of High Imperialism*, London.

Eichengreen, B. J. (1992) *Golden Fetters: The Gold Standard and the Great Depression, 1919–1939*, Oxford.

Ford, A. G. (1974) 'British Investment in Argentina and Long Swings,

1880–1914', in R. Floud (Ed.), *Essays in Quantitative Economic History*, Oxford.

Forrester, J. W. (1977) 'Growth Cycles', *The Economist*, 125, 525–43.

Forrester, J. W. (1978) 'Changing Economic Patterns', *Technology Review*, 80, 8.

Forrester, J. W. (1981) 'Innovation and Economic Change', *Futures*, 13, 323–31.

Freeman, C., Clark, J. and Soete, J. (1982) *Unemployment and Technical Innovation: A Study of Long Waves and Economic Development*, London.

Friedman, M. and Schwartz, A. J. (1982) *Monetary Trends in the United States and the United Kingdom*, Chicago.

Garvy, G. (1943) 'Kondratieff's Theory of Long Waves', *Review of Economic Statistics*, 25, 203–19.

Gerschenkron, A. (1962) *Economic Backwardness in Historical Perspective*, New York.

Graham, A. K. and Senge, M. (1980) 'A Long Wave Hypothesis of Innovation', *Technological Forecasting and Social Change*, 17, 283–311.

Harkness, J. P. (1968) 'A Spectral–Analytic Test of the Long Swing Hypothesis in Canada', *Review of Economics and Statistics*, 50, 429–36.

Hickman, B. G. (1963) 'Postwar Growth in the US in the Light of the Long Swing Hypothesis', *American Economic Review, Papers and Proceedings*, 53, 490–507.

Hickman, B. G. (1974) 'What Became of the Building Cycle?', in P. David and M. Reder (Eds), *Nations and Households in Economic Growth: Essays in Honor of Moses Abramovitz*, New York.

Hoffmann, W. G. (1965) *Das Wachstum der Deutschen Wirtschaft seit der Mitte Das 19 Jahrhunderts*, Berlin.

Howrey, E. P. (1968) 'A Spectrum Analysis of the Long Swing Hypothesis', *International Economic Review*, 9, 228–52.

Isard, W. (1942) 'A Neglected Cycle: The Transport–Building Cycle', *Review of Economic Statistics*, 24, 149–58.

Jewkes, J., Sawers, D. and Stillerman, R. (1969) *The Sources of Invention*, London.

Kindleberger, C. P. (1955) 'Industrial Europe's Terms of Trade on Current Account, 1870–1953', *Economic Journal*, 65, 19–35.

Kindleberger, C. P. (1983) *The World in Depression 1929–1939*, London.

Kleinknecht, A. (1987) *Innovation Patterns in Crisis and Prosperity: Schumpeter's Long Cycle Reconsidered*, London.

Klolz, B. P. (1973) 'Oscillatory Growth in Three Nations', *Journal of the American Statistical Association*, 68, 562–7.

Klolz, B. P. and Neal, L. (1973) 'Spectral and Cross Spectral Analysis of the Long Swing Hypothesis', *Review of Economics and Statistics*, 55, 291–8.

Kondratieff, N. D. (1922) *Mirovoe khozyaistvo i ego kon'iunktury vo vremia i posle voiny*, Volgada.

Kondratieff, N. D. (1924) 'On the Notion of Economic Statics, Dynamics, and Fluctuations', *Sotsialisticheskoe Khoziaistvo*, 2, 349–82. An abridged English translation appears as 'The Static and Dynamic View of Economics' (1925), *Quarterly Journal of Economics*, 39, 575–83.

Kondratieff, N. D. (1925) 'The Major Economic Cycles', *Voprosy kon'iunktury*, 1, 28–79. An abridged English translation appears as 'The Long Waves in Economic Life' (1935), *Review of Economic Statistics*, 17, 105–15. A complete translation (1979) can be found in *Review*, 2, 519–62.

Kondratieff, N. D. and Oparin, D. I. (1928) *Bol'shie tsikly kon'yunktury*, Moscow. An English translation (1984) appears as *The Long Wave Cycle*, New York.

Kuczynski, Th. (1978) 'Spectral Analysis and Cluster Analysis as Mathematical Methods for the Periodisation of Historical Processes. A Comparison of Results Based on Data about the Development of Production and Innovation in the History of Capitalism. Kondratieff Cycles Appearance or Reality?', Paper for the Seventh International Economic History Congress, Edinburgh.

Kuczynski, Th. (1980) 'Have There Been Differences Between the Growth Rates in Different Periods of the Capitalist World Economy since 1850? An Application of Cluster Analysis in Time Series Analysis', in J. M. Clubb and E. K. Scheuch (Eds), *Historical Social Research of Historical and Process-Produced Data*, Stuttgart.

Kuznets, S. S. (1930) *Secular Movements in Production and Prices: Their Nature and Their Bearing upon Cyclical Fluctuations*, Cambridge, Mass.

Kuznets, S. S. (1940) 'Schumpeter's Business Cycles', *American Economic Review*, 30, 257–71.

Kuznets, S. S. (1952) 'Long Term Changes in the National Income of the USA since 1870'. in S. Kuznets (Ed.), *Income and Wealth of the United States*, Cambridge.

Kuznets, S. S. (1958) 'Long Swings in the Growth of Population and in Related Economic Variables', *Proceedings of the American Philosophical Society*, 102, 25–52.

Lévy-Leboyer, M. (1978) 'Capital Investment and Economic Growth in France', in P. Mathias and M. M. Postan (Eds), *The Cambridge Economic History of Europe*, Vol. 7, Cambridge.

Lewis, W. A. (1952) 'World Production, Prices and Trade', *Manchester School*, 20, 105–38.

Lewis, W. A. (1978) *Growth and Fluctuations 1870–1913*, London.

Lewis, W. A. (1981) 'The Rate of Growth of World Trade, 1830–1973', in S. Grassmann and E. Lundberg (Eds), *The World Economic Order*, London.

Lewis, W. A. and O'Leary, P. J. (1955) 'Secular Swings in Production and Trade, 1870–1913', *Manchester School*, 23, 113–52.

Maddison, A. (1982) *Phases of Capitalist Development*, Oxford.

Maddison, A. (1991) *Dynamic Forces in Capitalist Development*, Oxford.

Mandel, E. (1980) *Long Waves of Capitalist Development: The Marxist Interpretation*, Cambridge.

Matthews, R. C. O., Feinstein, C. and Odling-Smee, J. (1982) *British Economic Growth*, Oxford.

Mensch, G. (1979) *Stalemate in Technology: Innovations Overcome the Depression*, Cambridge, Mass.

Metz, R. (1992) 'A Re-examination of Long Waves in Aggregate Production Series', in A. Kleinknecht, E. Mandel and I. Wallerstein (Eds), *New Findings in Long-Wave Research*, London.

Metz, R. and Spree, R. (1981) 'Kuznets–Zyklen im Wachstum der deutschen Wirtshaftwahrend des 19. und fruhen 20. Jahrhunderts', in D. Petzina and G. van Roon (Eds), *Konjunktur, Krise, Gesellschaft*, Stuttgart.

Minami, R. (1986) *The Economic Development of Japan: A Quantitative Study*, London.

Minsky, H. P. (1964) 'Longer Waves in Financial Relations: Financial Factors in the More Severe Depressions', *American Economic Review, Papers and Proceedings*, 54, 324–35.

Ohkawa, K. and Rosovsky, H. (1973) *Japanese Economic Growth: Trend Acceleration in the Twentieth Century*, Stanford.

Parry-Lewis, J. (1964) 'Growth and Inverse Cycles: A Two Country Model', *Economic Journal*, 74, 109–18.

Pope, D. (1984) 'Rostow's Kondratieff Cycle in Australia', *Journal of Economic History*, 44, 729–53.

Reijnders, J. P. G. (1992) 'Between Trends and Trade Cycles: Kondratieff

Long Waves Revisited', in A. Kleinknecht, E. Mandel and I. Wallerstein (Eds), *New Findings in Long-Wave Research*, London.

Romer, C. (1986) 'New Estimates of Prewar GNP and Unemployment', *Journal of Economic History*, 2, 341–52.

Rosenberg, N. and Frischtak, C. R. (1983) 'Long Waves and Economic Growth: A Critical Appraisal', *American Economic Review*, 73, 146–51.

Rostow, W. W. (1975) 'Kondratieff, Schumpeter, and Kuznets: Trend Periods Revisited', *Journal of Economic History*, 35, 719–53.

Rostow, W. W. (1978) *The World Economy*, London.

Rostow, W. W. and Kennedy, M. (1979) 'A Simple Model of the Kondratieff Cycle', *Research in Economic History*, 4, 1–36.

Sahal, D. (1980) 'The Nature and Significance of Technological Cycles', *International Journal of Systems Science*, 11, 985–1000.

Samuels, W. and Makasheva, N. (Eds) (1998) *The Works of Nikolai Kondratiev*, London.

Schumpeter, J. A. (1935) 'The Analysis of Economic Change', *Review of Economic Statistics*, 17, 2–10.

Schumpeter, J. A. (1939) *Business Cycles: A Theoretical, Historical and Statistical Analysis of the Capitalist Process*, New York.

Schumpeter, J. A. (1950) *Capitalism, Socialism and Democracy*, New York.

Slutsky, E. (1937) 'The Summation of Random Causes as the Cause of Cyclical Processes', *Econometrica*, 5, 105–46.

Solomou, S. N. (1986a) 'Non-Balanced Growth and Kondratieff Waves in the World Economy, 1850–1913', *Journal of Economic History*, 46, 165–71.

Solomou, S. N. (1986b) 'Innovation Clusters and Kondratieff Long Waves in Economic Growth', *Cambridge Journal of Economics*, 10, 101–12.

Solomou, S. N. (1987) *Phases of Economic Growth 1850–1973: Kondratieff Waves and Kuznets Swings*, Cambridge.

Soper, J. C. (1975) 'Myth and Reality in Economic Time Series: The Long Swing Revisited', *Southern Economic Journal*, 4, 570–9.

Soper, J. C. (1978) *The Long Swing in Historical Perspective*, New York.

Thomas, B. (1954) *Migration and Economic Growth*, revised edition (1973), Cambridge.

Thomas, B. (1973) *Migration and Urban Development: A Reappraisal of British and American Long Cycles*, London.

Van der Zwan, A. (1980) 'On the Assessment of the Kondratieff Cycle and Related Issues', in S. K. Kuipers, and G. J. Lanjouw (Eds), *Prospects of Economic Growth*, Amsterdam.

Van Duijn, J. J. (1977) 'The Long Wave in Economic Life', *De Economist*, 125, 544–76.

Van Duijn, J. J. (1981) 'Fluctuations in Innovations Over Time', *Futures*, 13, 264–75.

Van Duijn, J. J. (1983) *The Long Wave in Economic Life*, London.

Van Ewijk, C. (1981) 'The Long Wave a Real Phenomenon?', *The Economist*, 129, 324–72.

Williamson, J. G. (1984) 'Why Was British Growth So Slow During the Industrial Revolution?', *Journal of Economic History*, 42, 687–712.

Chapter 4

Lessons and conclusions

Cyclical regularities

There has been a tendency among economists and economic historians to analyse business cycles in the context of regular stylised facts. The evidence considered suggests that many of the defining features of business cycles are time specific. The mean durations and amplitudes, the persistence profiles of shocks and causal processes behind business cycles have all changed significantly over time. The strongest statement that can be made on the issue of business cycle regularities is that some common features can be observed over a number of historical periods. This suggests that specific patterns of adjustment seem to emerge only within particular epochs.

Fixed exchange rates and business cycle stability

One feature of interest in terms of the current and future policy agenda is that business cycle volatility has been significantly less under fixed exchange rate eras (such as the classical gold standard and Bretton Woods) than under more volatile exchange rate experiences (such as the inter-war period). The evidence considered suggests that volatility is not a simple outcome of the exchange rate regime. The recent literature has shown that the stability of the gold standard era should be attributed to the existence of viable adjustment mechanisms rather than to the fixed exchange rate regime in itself. Given the historical uniqueness of the adjustment mechanisms observed over the period 1870–1913, it is clear that we cannot generate the same stability in the future by simply instituting a fixed exchange rate regime or a single currency. At most we can argue that the institutional arrangements of the classical gold standard era and Bretton Woods gave rise to a dampening effect on business cycle amplitudes by imposing constraints on monetary and fiscal policy discretion.

Money and business cycles

Recent business cycle discussions have been conducted along the lines of evaluating the empirical validity of real business cycle theory relative to monetary theory. By restricting the evidence to the post-war era many of the results can be highly misleading as general policy guides. The evidence considered suggests that we need to distinguish the role of monetary policy shocks under different policy regimes and institutional structures. Hence, monetary policy shocks were *relatively* more important in the inter-war era than in the classical gold standard period; similarly, monetary shocks have been more important since 1973 than in the Bretton Woods era. To dismiss the role of money in business cycle fluctuations based on the results of studies of the early post-war period, as the recent real business cycle perspectives have done, is again highly misleading as a general policy guide. The evidence for the whole period since 1870 suggests that monetary (and financial) shocks have been important to cyclical fluctuations. The occurrence and effect of such shocks can be related to the monetary institutions and the nature of the international payments system.

Real business cycle shocks

Real shocks have had an important impact on business cycle fluctuations. The type of shocks have, however, changed over time.

For example, during 1870–1913 supply-side shocks to the agricultural sector were still important to business cycle fluctuations. Technology shocks have also been emphasised in much of the recent theoretical literature. However, far more work is needed to identify the sectoral supply-side shocks contributing to aggregate fluctuations if this approach is going to lead to useful empirical insights. What is clear is that the polarisation of the recent debates into an either/or explanation of monetary and real business cycle theory is both unnecessary and misleading. Both types of shock are encompassed within an impulse theory of business cycles: the aim of a research agenda should be to determine the specific mix of shocks which has varied as a result of structural change and policy regime changes. Understanding why the mix of shocks has varied over time or policy regimes is an important issue. In formulating conditional predictions about the future, an informed understanding of the past suggests that the mix of monetary and real shocks will vary in the light of institutional and structural change.

Long economic fluctuations

Irregular (stochastic) long cycles have been observed in modern economies. Two types of long duration fluctuations have been observed. First, there has been an irregular long cycle in the performance of world trade and production since 1870. This is not equivalent to arguing that endogenous Kondratieff waves describe world economic development: however, a series of impulses to world institutions have propagated a cyclical pattern in world economic growth. Secondly, a long duration cycle has been observed at the national level over some historical periods. National long swings were pervasive during the period 1870–1913. The propagation mechanisms and shocks generating such swings are linked to the fixed exchange rate regime and the type of adjustments that were possible before 1914. A fixed exchange rate regime imposed a rules-driven policy framework on participants, constraining the response to national-specific shocks. In time of adverse shocks, high levels of international labour and capital mobility helped the adjustment path by reducing the required level of deflation.

As different regional blocs attempt to re-establish fixed exchange rate regimes and single currency areas in the future, the adjustment to shocks will once again become policy constrained. For example, Europe's commitment to a single currency under economic and monetary union implies that migration flows will have to act as an important equilibrating mechanism to national-specific shocks if we are not to observe persistent divergence across different countries. Such flows will generate the *possibility* of slow adjusting economic–demographic interactions on the cyclical process, which has clear homologies with the gold standard pattern of international adjustments. Such migration flows are not inevitable. The lesson to be learnt is that for institutions to endure they need viable adjustment mechanisms: the Kuznets swings that arose out of the adjustment mechanisms of the classical gold standard period will need to be recreated by encouraging capital and migration flows.

Theory and history of business cycles

It is clear that impulse theories of business cycles, such as the recent monetary and real business cycle theories, have serious empirical and theoretical limitations in their attempts to account for business cycle phenomena. In developing theories of cycles we clearly need to incorporate as much as possible of the empirical/historical evidence available to us. One of the key limitations of recent business cycle theory has been the attempt to account for post-war stylised facts: paradoxically this becomes an exercise in recent economic history rather than the formation of a convincing theory based on long-run evidence. The many changes in cyclical features reflect, among other things, changes to economic structures, policy frameworks and behavioural patterns. Given that these features are in a state of flux we are unlikely to observe a universal business cycle structure that can be understood by explaining the features of particular periods. The theory of business cycles needs to integrate history if it is to provide meaningful (conditional) statements about the future. We cannot hope to predict business cycles, but we can hope to understand the foundations for making conditional predictions.

The end of business cycles?

The idea that business cycles can come to an end seems naive. Today we realise that economic fluctuations are part of economic life. Moreover, as we have a better understanding of concepts of equilibrium in economics, it is clear that the path of business cycles is not predictable.

Glossary

Terms appearing in bold in the text are explained in this glossary.

Accelerator theory

This is a theory of investment determination. The simple 'naive' accelerator models the level of investment as being determined by the change in aggregate output:

$$I = v \, (Y_t - Y_{t-1})$$

where:

I = level of investment,
Y = level of output,
v = constant.

As a simplifying assumption this relationship is often specified as a linear relationship, where the parameter v is constant.

Adjustable peg

In an adjustable peg system of international payments the expectation is that nominal exchange rates are *normally* fixed but countries are allowed to alter their exchange rates, if circumstances require. This system operated under the Bretton

Woods arrangements for the period after World War II until 1972. Countries agreed to fix their exchange rates against the dollar, creating an adjustable peg around a dollar standard.

Amplitude

This is a measure of the variance of a cycle. Peak to trough changes in variables such as output and prices are usually used to describe the amplitude of a particular depression.

Balanced budget

Refers to a fiscal expansion that is fully financed by tax increases.

Bretton Woods

The international agreement resulting from the 1944 conference held at Bretton Woods (in the US) to discuss alternative proposals from the US, Britain and Canada for setting up new international institutions. The agreement set up the International Monetary Fund and the World Bank. The two key aims of these new institutions were stable exchange rates and the provision of sufficient finance for post-war reconstruction.

Contra-cyclical

See Pro-cyclical patterns.

Core industrial countries

Refers to the group of major industrial countries. During the period 1870–1913 most of world production and trade in manufactured goods was accounted by four countries (the US, Britain, France and Germany). During the twentieth century the number of major industrial countries has increased significantly.

Core–periphery trade

Refers to the trade between the major industrial countries and countries specialising in the production of primary commodities. This has also been referred to as north–south trade.

Demand-side shocks/demand management

Shocks to the economy resulting from government monetary and fiscal policy. Demand management is the use of fiscal and monetary policy to influence the state of aggregate demand in the economy.

Discretion-driven system

See Rules-driven policy framework.

Effective exchange rate

An index of exchange rates relating one currency to a basket of other currencies. Weights can be taken from either bilateral trade shares or shares of world trade. If nominal rates are adjusted for relative price changes across countries the index constructed is referred to as a *real* effective exchange rate.

Gold exchange standard

A system of international payments which values currencies at fixed amounts of gold or of other currencies fixed to gold. Under this system paper currency is not convertible into gold but into the currency of some other country on the gold standard. A gold exchange standard was operating during 1925–31, with the dollar playing an important role as a reserve currency.

Gold standard

A system of international payments that values currencies at fixed amounts of gold. All the major industrial counties (Britain, France, Germany and the US) operated a gold standard during 1879–1913. However, even during this period a gold exchange standard was evolving, with sterling increasingly acting as reserve currency.

Granger causality

A variable x 'Granger causes' another variable y if past values of x explain the current value of y. For example, if past values of money supply variations cause current values of gross domestic product we would argue that money supply variations have a causal effect on gross domestic product.

Growth cycle

During the post-war 'golden age' (1950–73), business cycle fluctuations manifested themselves as variations in the rate of economic growth rather than level changes to production, which had been the norm before the war. Thus, a retardation of economic growth below trend was referred to as a recession and a growth rate above trend was referred to as a boom.

Hodrick–Prescott (H–P) filter

The H–P filter sets out an algorithm which endogenously determines the trend of a variable, encompassing linear and stochastic trends. Deviations about the trend are taken to depict cyclical fluctuations. The filter has been used extensively in recent real business cycle discussions.

Intra-industry trade

This refers to the trade of similar commodities across countries (for example, British cars traded for Japanese cars). The twentieth century has seen an expansion of intra-industry trade, which is also reflected in new regional trading patterns (for example, intra-European trade has expanded rapidly).

Inventory cycle (Kitchin cycle)

A short cycle with a length of two to four years. Kitchin (1923) observed the cycle in a study of bank clearings and prices. Kitchin attributed the observed cycle to shocks that cause adjustments to inventory stocks.

Kondratieff wave

A cycle of prices and output with an approximate periodicity of 50–60 years. The upswing of the cycle represents a phase of rapid economic growth lasting between 20 and 30 years; the downswing of the cycle shows retardation in economic growth of a similar duration.

Kuznets swing

A cycle in economic growth that is approximately 20 years in duration. The actual length of the swings found varies with different authors, ranging between 14 and 22 years. The cycle is named after Simon Kuznets, who was one of the first economists to observe the phenomenon in his studies of the US economy (Kuznets, 1930).

Long swing

See Kuznets swings.

Non-trend-stationary

If the movement of a variable, once shocked away from equilibrium, does not revert back to a well defined trend value, it is said to be non-trend-stationary. The variable tends to drift away from a mean value. The specific path of a variable is dependent on the nature of historical shocks. This is also referred to as a random walk.

Primary producer

Refers to a country or sector within a country with a trade and production specialisation that is concentrated in agricultural or raw material commodities.

Pro-cyclical patterns

Variables that move in the same direction over the business cycle are described as pro-cyclical. For example, real wages move pro-cyclically with employment if real wage increases are associated with rising employment. If variables move inversely over the business cycle their relationship is described as contra-cyclical. For example, if prices and output move contra-cyclically, price rises are associated with cyclical downturns.

Random walk

See Non-trend-stationary.

Real business cycle shock

A shock that shifts the production function. Technological and weather shocks are good examples of such shocks.

Reference cycle

Reference cycles capture the peaks and troughs in general business conditions. The methodology was developed by Wesley Mitchell and Willard Thorp at the National Bureau of Economic Research and was applied to a number of the major industrial countries. Using information from contemporary press reports and a wide set of quantitative variables, the peak and trough dating was intended to provide a picture of aggregate business cycle conditions.

Rules-driven policy framework

If governments agree to abide by rules that they cannot easily change, the policy regime may be referred to as rules driven. For example, abiding by the rules of the gold standard meant accepting constraints on the use of monetary and fiscal policies. The other extreme of policy formation is a discretion-driven system. The establishment of economic and monetary union in Europe will push Europe towards a rules-driven policy framework.

'S'-shaped growth trajectory

This refers to a growth process going through a number of stages. A period of slow growth is followed by a period of accelerated growth. This is followed by a phase of maturity when growth rates begin to level off and gradually decline. The idea has been used to depict product life cycles but it has also been used to model national economic performance.

Terms of trade

The ratio of export prices to import prices (often referred to as the net barter terms of trade). If export prices rise faster than import prices (or fall more slowly than import prices) the terms of trade are said to 'improve'. The gross terms of trade measure changes in the quantity relationship of exports and imports. This index is also referred to as the international terms of trade. If we are interested in sectoral relative prices (as between manufactured goods and primary commodities) we need to consider the ratio of the two sectoral price indices. This ratio is referred to as the sectoral terms of trade.

Total factor productivity

Refers to an index of output per unit of total factor input. If measured as a growth rate it refers to the growth of output minus the growth rate of total factor input. Total factor input is often defined as the weighted growth rate of capital and labour input, where the weights are derived from factor shares in national income.

Trade cycle

Also referred to as the Juglar cycle, this describes a cycle lasting eight to nine years. The cycle is named after Clement Juglar, who was one of the first trade cycle researchers to observe this periodicity, in the nineteenth century.

Trend-stationary paths

Describes a time-series that follows a well defined trend value. In the long run upward deviations will be followed by downward deviations. In this sense transitory shocks have transitory effects on the specific variable.

Vector autoregression (VAR)

A VAR model is a system of equations in which each variable is a function of past values of all other variables as well as of its own past values. These types of model have been used to analyse the issue of Granger causality in the economic system and the adjustment path of specific shocks.

Bibliography

Kitchin, J. (1923) 'Cycles and Trends in Economic Factors, *Review of Economic Statistics*, 5, 10–16.

Kuznets, S. S. (1930) *Secular Movements in Production and Prices: Their Nature and Their Bearing Upon Cyclical Fluctuations*, Cambridge, Mass.

Index